Virtual Networks Unlocked: Your Guide to Azure Connectivity

Kameron Hussain and Frahaan Hussain

Published by Sonar Publishing, 2025.

VIRTUAL NETWORKS UNLOCKED: YOUR GUIDE TO AZURE CONNECTIVITY

First edition. April 17, 2025.

ISBN: 979-8227304650

Written by Kameron Hussain and Frahaan Hussain.

Preface

In today's digital-first world, the cloud is more than a buzzword—it's a foundational pillar of modern IT. Whether you're an aspiring network engineer, a cloud architect, or an IT decision-maker, understanding cloud networking is essential to building robust, scalable, and secure infrastructures. **Microsoft Azure**, one of the leading cloud platforms, offers powerful networking capabilities designed to meet the demands of both startups and enterprises alike.

This book, *Virtual Networks Unlocked: Your Guide to Azure Connectivity*, serves as your practical guide to mastering Azure's virtual networking components and strategies. Starting with fundamental concepts, it gradually introduces real-world techniques and advanced architectures that align with the needs of today's hybrid and cloud-native environments.

Throughout this first edition, you'll learn how to:

- Establish secure and scalable **Virtual Networks (VNets)**
- Interconnect networks through **VNet Peering** and **Hybrid Connectivity**
- Protect your infrastructure with **Azure-native security tools**
- Monitor and troubleshoot your networks using **Azure Network Watcher**
- Automate network deployments using **ARM templates, Bicep, and PowerShell**

- Explore **real-world scenarios** from diverse industries such as SaaS, healthcare, and finance

Each chapter is structured to progressively build your expertise, supported with practical examples and configurations you can replicate in your own Azure environment. The goal is not just to explain *how*, but also *why*—providing context that empowers you to design with confidence.

By the end of this book, you will be equipped to architect, deploy, and manage Azure networks for a wide range of use cases, whether you're migrating from on-premises or starting natively in the cloud. Welcome to the journey—let's dive into the world of Azure Virtual Networking.

Chapter 1: Introduction to Azure Virtual Networking

What Is a Virtual Network (VNet)?

A **Virtual Network (VNet)** in Azure is a logically isolated section of the Microsoft Azure cloud dedicated to your subscription. It allows you to securely communicate with other Azure resources, the internet, and on-premises networks. VNets in Azure function much like traditional networks in an on-premises datacenter but come with added flexibility, scalability, and integration with Azure services.

At its core, a VNet provides a fundamental building block for private networking in the cloud. It's a **software-defined network (SDN)**, abstracted from the underlying hardware and capable of being provisioned, configured, and managed entirely through Azure's platform.

The purpose of a VNet is to allow **compute resources**, such as virtual machines (VMs), containers, and app services, to communicate securely with each other, with the internet, and with on-premises environments. Without a VNet, these resources would be isolated and unable to exchange data effectively.

VNets support:

- **Private IP Addressing**: Resources can communicate using internal IPs.
- **Subnets**: Logical segmentation of a VNet to enhance security and efficiency.
- **Route Tables**: Custom routing of traffic within and across VNets.
- **Network Security Groups (NSGs)**: Layered security via firewall-like rules.
- **Service Endpoints**: Secure access to Azure services without public IP exposure.
- **VNet Peering**: Seamless connectivity between VNets.
- **VPN Gateways and ExpressRoute**: Hybrid connectivity options to link Azure with on-premises.

In short, a VNet is your private network in Azure, acting as a flexible and powerful foundation upon which nearly all other Azure services can be deployed.

Azure Virtual Network vs. Traditional On-Premises Network

Feature	Traditional Network	Azure VNet
Hardware	Requires physical devices	Fully virtualized
Setup Time	Weeks to months	Minutes
Scalability	Limited by hardware	Virtually unlimited
Maintenance	Manual updates and monitoring	Azure-managed
Integration	Manual configurations for cloud	Built-in integration with Azure services

The abstraction layer Azure provides means network architects no longer need to deal with physical switches, cables, and firewalls. Everything can be defined in software, often as code, leading to repeatable, scalable deployments.

Core Components of a Virtual Network

Address Space

VNets use **IP address ranges** (in CIDR notation) to define the scope of their private address space. For example, 10.0.0.0/16 defines an address space that allows for 65,536 IP addresses.

Example of defining a VNet in Azure CLI

az network vnet create \

—name MyVNet \

—resource-group MyResourceGroup \

—location eastus \

—address-prefix 10.0.0.0/16

This IP range is divided among **subnets** within the VNet.

Subnets

Subnets divide the VNet into smaller address spaces, enhancing security and network management. Subnetting allows for the isolation of resources based on functionality or role. For instance:

- 10.0.1.0/24 – Web Servers
- 10.0.2.0/24 – Application Servers
- 10.0.3.0/24 – Database Servers

Each subnet can have its own **route table** and **NSG**, providing fine-grained control over traffic.

Network Security Groups (NSGs)

NSGs act like firewalls that allow or deny inbound/outbound traffic based on rules. These rules can be applied at the **subnet** or **NIC (network interface card)** level.

Example rule:

- Allow inbound HTTP traffic (port 80) from internet
- Deny all inbound traffic except specific ports

NSGs support:

- Protocol (TCP, UDP)

- Source/Destination IPs
- Port ranges
- Priorities

Route Tables

Azure provides system routes by default, but you can override them using **User-Defined Routes (UDRs)**. This allows for scenarios like directing traffic to a **firewall, NVA (Network Virtual Appliance)**, or **VPN gateway**.

Example route:

- Destination: 0.0.0.0/0
- Next hop: Virtual Appliance (10.0.1.4)

DNS Integration

VNets integrate with **Azure-provided DNS** or custom DNS servers. This allows for name resolution within the VNet or across hybrid networks.

Service Endpoints and Private Link

Service Endpoints extend your VNet to Azure services like Storage or SQL Database over the Microsoft backbone network, eliminating the need to traverse the internet.

Private Link allows access to services through a private IP in your VNet, adding an extra layer of security.

VNet Isolation and Multi-Tenancy

Each VNet is **isolated** by default, meaning resources in one VNet cannot communicate with another unless explicitly connected using **VNet peering** or **VPNs**. This is crucial for **multi-tenant environments** where segregation of workloads is required.

You can create multiple VNets in a subscription and manage access using **Azure RBAC**, **NSGs**, and **Azure Policy**.

Benefits of Using Azure VNets

- **Scalability**: Easily scale from a single subnet to large, complex topologies.
- **Security**: Control traffic flow with NSGs, route tables, and firewalls.
- **Integration**: Native support for Azure services like Azure SQL, App Service, and AKS.
- **Hybrid Compatibility**: Seamless connectivity to on-premises environments.
- **Automation**: Full support for deployment using ARM, Bicep, CLI, PowerShell, and Terraform.

Common Scenarios Where VNets Are Used

1. **Hosting Web Applications** with secure back-end services.
2. **Running Containerized Workloads** using Azure Kubernetes Service (AKS).
3. **Connecting Branch Offices** to Azure via VPN or ExpressRoute.
4. **Isolating Dev/Test Environments** from Production.

5. **Compliance-Driven Deployments** with strict network segmentation.

Summary

Azure Virtual Networks are the cornerstone of every cloud architecture built on Microsoft Azure. They offer the same control and security as a traditional network but with cloud agility and scalability. By mastering VNets, you lay the groundwork for implementing advanced solutions like hybrid connectivity, microservices deployments, and secure enterprise-grade systems.

As we move into Chapter 2, you'll learn how to create your first VNet using the Azure Portal, set up subnets, configure network security, and begin building a robust, production-ready virtual network environment.

Importance of Cloud Connectivity

In the age of digital transformation, cloud computing is no longer a futuristic concept—it is the present. Organizations across industries are migrating workloads to cloud environments to increase agility, reduce costs, and drive innovation. However, the effectiveness of cloud computing hinges on one critical factor: **connectivity**. Without secure, reliable, and performant connections to and within the cloud, the advantages of cloud infrastructure cannot be fully realized.

Cloud connectivity refers to the ability of services, applications, and devices—whether on-premises, in the cloud, or at the edge—to communicate efficiently and securely over the network. In the Azure ecosystem, connectivity underpins nearly every architecture, enabling resources to work together cohesively regardless of physical location.

This section explores the **strategic importance of cloud connectivity**, the various methods of establishing and optimizing connections in Azure, and how virtual networking plays a central role in achieving seamless integration between services and systems.

The Role of Connectivity in Cloud-First Architectures

As enterprises shift from traditional monolithic architectures to distributed, microservices-based, and cloud-native solutions, the network becomes the backbone that ties everything together. Every modern cloud-first design relies on consistent, secure, and high-throughput network communication.

Key Scenarios Requiring Strong Cloud Connectivity

1. **Hybrid Deployments**: On-premises data centers connected to Azure to support lift-and-shift migrations or hybrid applications.
2. **Global Reach**: Applications with users and resources spread across multiple geographies.
3. **IoT and Edge Computing**: Devices at the edge uploading telemetry data to cloud-based analytics engines.
4. **Business Continuity and Disaster Recovery (BCDR)**: Replication and failover mechanisms that span cloud and on-premises regions.
5. **Security and Compliance**: Enforcing data flows through specific inspection points (e.g., firewalls, DLP systems).

In each of these scenarios, connectivity is not just a technical requirement—it becomes a **strategic enabler** of business continuity, performance, and security.

Azure's Networking Philosophy

Azure's networking stack is designed with five guiding principles:

1. **Security** – Default-deny posture, encryption in transit, and strong identity control.
2. **Performance** – Low-latency, high-throughput backbone with global scale.
3. **Availability** – Redundant links, zones, and regions to maintain uptime.
4. **Simplicity** – Intuitive configuration interfaces, templates, and automation support.
5. **Flexibility** – Multiple connection types and topologies tailored to diverse needs.

Understanding these principles helps contextualize why certain Azure networking features are designed the way they are and how to best leverage them.

Types of Cloud Connectivity in Azure

Azure offers multiple layers and types of connectivity options to address a wide spectrum of use cases. These include:

Intra-VNet Connectivity

This refers to traffic between resources (e.g., virtual machines, containers, app services) within the same Virtual Network. Azure provides automatic, seamless internal routing between these resources using private IP addresses.

No special configuration is required beyond ensuring the resources reside in the same VNet and subnet or are allowed to communicate across subnets (i.e., no NSG rules block the traffic).

Inter-VNet Connectivity

In scenarios where resources are in different VNets—either in the same or different regions—**VNet peering** is used. Peering creates a low-latency, high-bandwidth connection between VNets and supports transitive routing under specific configurations.

Example:

```
# Peer VNet1 and VNet2

az network vnet peering create \

—name VNet1-to-VNet2 \

—resource-group MyResourceGroup \

—vnet-name VNet1 \

—remote-vnet VNet2 \

—allow-vnet-access
```

This allows seamless communication without relying on public IPs or external routing.

On-Premises to Azure Connectivity

1. **Point-to-Site VPN**: Ideal for individual users or remote offices. Establishes a secure connection from a client machine to Azure using certificates or RADIUS authentication.
2. **Site-to-Site VPN**: Connects an entire on-premises network to Azure via an IPsec tunnel. Suitable for consistent, moderate-throughput use cases.
3. **Azure ExpressRoute**: Provides a private, dedicated fiber

link between on-premises infrastructure and Azure datacenters. Offers guaranteed bandwidth, low latency, and is not routed over the public internet.

Each of these options can coexist in hybrid scenarios depending on performance, availability, and security requirements.

Internet Connectivity

Azure resources can access the internet either by default (e.g., outbound internet connectivity for VMs without a public IP) or explicitly via **public IP addresses**, **NAT gateways**, and **application gateways**.

However, exposing resources directly to the internet is discouraged unless absolutely necessary. Prefer **Azure Front Door**, **Application Gateway with WAF**, or **Private Link** for public access scenarios.

Connectivity to Azure Services

Azure provides two mechanisms to improve connectivity to platform services (like Azure SQL, Blob Storage, etc.):

- **Service Endpoints**: Extend your VNet to Azure services. Improves performance and security but still relies on public IP addresses behind the scenes.

- **Private Link**: Maps an Azure service to a private IP within your VNet. Traffic remains entirely within the Microsoft backbone network, enabling secure access without internet exposure.

These features are crucial for meeting security and compliance requirements while maintaining high performance.

Performance and Reliability Considerations

Azure Global Network

Azure operates one of the largest **SD-WAN**-based backbone networks in the world, connecting its datacenters across 60+ regions via private fiber infrastructure. This network enables:

- Minimal latency between regions
- High throughput
- Built-in redundancy and failover mechanisms

When designing for performance, it is vital to:

- Place related services in the same region or availability zone where possible.
- Use **Availability Sets** or **Availability Zones** to ensure resilience.
- Leverage **Load Balancers** and **Traffic Manager** for regional or global distribution.
- Optimize DNS with **Azure DNS** or **Traffic Manager** for geo-redundancy and latency-based routing.

Monitoring Network Performance

To ensure optimal performance and fast fault resolution, Azure provides:

- **Azure Network Watcher**: Monitor, diagnose, and gain insights into network traffic and health.

- **Connection Monitor**: Check the status of connectivity between endpoints.

- **Metrics and Logs**: Gather throughput, latency, packet loss, and other indicators to fine-tune your network design.

Security and Governance in Connectivity

Connectivity introduces risk. Every open port, peer, or VPN tunnel is a potential attack vector. Thus, securing cloud connectivity must be a top priority.

Key Security Controls

- **Network Security Groups (NSGs)**: Define granular rules for traffic flow.

- **Application Security Groups (ASGs)**: Simplify NSG rules by grouping resources.

- **Azure Firewall**: Stateful inspection, high availability, and central policy management.

- **Web Application Firewall (WAF)**: Protect against OWASP Top 10 threats.

- **DDoS Protection**: Auto-enabled basic protection, with standard plans for enterprises.

- **Zero Trust Model**: Never trust, always verify—apply identity and policy checks at every step.

Implementing **Network Segmentation**, **least privilege**, and **role-based access control** ensures that connectivity does not compromise security.

Business Impact of Effective Cloud Connectivity

A well-architected connectivity strategy brings tangible business benefits:

- **Faster Time to Market**: Rapid, reproducible network deployments accelerate development and testing.

- **Improved User Experience**: Low-latency, optimized connections ensure smooth application performance.

- **Operational Continuity**: Redundant paths and automated failover protect against outages.

- **Regulatory Compliance**: Secure, auditable network traffic flow helps meet GDPR, HIPAA, and ISO standards.

- **Cost Optimization**: Efficient traffic routing, peering, and bandwidth management minimize spend.

Poor connectivity, on the other hand, can lead to service degradation, data breaches, compliance failures, and reputational damage.

Future Trends in Cloud Connectivity

As cloud technology evolves, so do the patterns of connectivity:

- **5G and Edge Integration**: Low-latency connections to devices and edge compute resources.
- **Software-Defined Networking (SDN)**: Dynamic, policy-driven control of networks.
- **AI-Powered Network Optimization**: Predictive analytics to optimize routing and performance.
- **Zero Trust Network Access (ZTNA)**: Replacing traditional VPNs with identity-centric access.

Azure is investing heavily in these technologies, making it imperative for professionals to understand and stay ahead of these trends.

Summary

Cloud connectivity is not merely a configuration step—it is a **strategic pillar** of modern cloud architecture. In the Azure ecosystem, robust networking ensures that applications are performant, secure, and resilient. From basic VNet setups to complex hybrid deployments and global scale-out solutions, understanding and designing for connectivity is what separates ad hoc implementations from enterprise-grade architectures.

In the next section, we'll explore Azure's networking capabilities in greater depth, including a breakdown of service offerings, integration points, and how they align with various workload requirements. This foundation will equip you to architect scalable, secure, and intelligent networks tailored to your organization's goals.

Overview of Azure Networking Capabilities

Azure offers a comprehensive suite of networking services designed to meet the needs of modern cloud-based applications. From simple virtual networks to complex hybrid infrastructures and global multi-region architectures, Azure's networking stack enables organizations to connect, secure, scale, and optimize their workloads. These capabilities are delivered through a rich set of tools and services, all of which are deeply integrated with the broader Azure ecosystem.

In this section, we will explore the key networking capabilities provided by Azure, categorized into logical areas such as connectivity, security, performance, automation, and monitoring. Understanding these services and their interrelationships is crucial for designing robust and future-proof cloud network architectures.

Core Connectivity Services

At the foundation of Azure networking lies the **Virtual Network (VNet)**. VNets provide the building blocks for private communication in Azure, enabling resources like virtual machines, databases, and containers to securely communicate with each other.

Virtual Network (VNet)

A VNet is a software-defined network that supports the following core functionalities:

- IP address assignment using CIDR blocks
- Subnet creation and management
- Intra- and inter-subnet communication

- Isolation and segmentation
- Integration with other Azure networking features like NSGs, route tables, and peering

Each VNet exists in a specific Azure region and subscription but can connect across regions through peering or global routing services.

Subnets

Subnets divide a VNet into smaller address spaces for organizational, security, or functional purposes. Subnets support:

- Logical grouping of resources
- Application of NSGs for traffic control
- User-defined route tables for custom routing behavior

By leveraging subnets, organizations can enforce least-privilege access and maintain better traffic visibility and control.

VNet Peering

Azure allows you to connect two VNets using **VNet Peering**. This enables seamless connectivity across different VNets without requiring a VPN gateway or public internet exposure.

Peering types:

- **Regional Peering**: Connects VNets within the same Azure region.

- **Global Peering**: Connects VNets across different Azure regions.

Peering is low-latency and high-bandwidth, leveraging Azure's internal backbone.

az network vnet peering create \

—name Peer1To2 \

—resource-group MyGroup \

—vnet-name VNet1 \

—remote-vnet VNet2 \

—allow-vnet-access

Virtual Network Gateway

To facilitate hybrid connectivity, Azure offers **Virtual Network Gateways** that support:

- **Site-to-Site VPNs**
- **Point-to-Site VPNs**
- **ExpressRoute connections**

These gateways allow encrypted connections between Azure and on-premises networks or branch locations.

ExpressRoute

ExpressRoute is Azure's premium private connectivity solution that bypasses the public internet entirely. It offers:

- Dedicated private link
- High throughput (up to 10 Gbps and beyond)
- SLA-backed reliability
- Layer 3 connectivity with global reach

It is ideal for enterprise workloads requiring guaranteed performance and regulatory compliance.

Load Balancing and Traffic Distribution

Azure provides multiple services for distributing traffic both within and across regions, improving performance, availability, and scalability.

Azure Load Balancer

A Layer 4 load balancer that distributes TCP/UDP traffic across backend resources. Key features:

- Supports both public and internal scenarios
- Automatically scales based on traffic
- Works with VMs, scale sets, and availability sets

Example usage:

- Distributing traffic across web servers in a single region
- Routing internal requests across microservices within a subnet

Azure Application Gateway

A Layer 7 (HTTP/HTTPS) load balancer with advanced routing capabilities, SSL termination, and integration with the **Web Application Firewall (WAF).**

Use cases include:

- Routing requests based on URL paths or host headers
- Protecting applications from common web vulnerabilities
- Terminating SSL at the edge for performance and simplicity

Azure Front Door

Azure Front Door is a globally distributed entry point for web applications. It provides:

- Global HTTP load balancing
- SSL offloading
- Application acceleration (via caching and anycast routing)
- URL-based routing and health probes

Front Door improves performance for globally distributed users and acts as a content delivery optimizer.

Azure Traffic Manager

DNS-based traffic distribution that enables geo-routing, weighted round-robin, and failover scenarios. It does not route traffic itself but resolves DNS queries based on configuration.

Best for:

- Directing users to the nearest available endpoint
- Regional failover and availability strategies
- Performance-optimized DNS-based routing

Security and Access Control

Azure's networking stack includes built-in security features that ensure traffic flows only where and how it should.

Network Security Groups (NSGs)

NSGs are stateful firewalls that control ingress and egress traffic at the subnet or NIC level. They use rule-based policies to filter traffic by:

- Source and destination IP
- Port range
- Protocol (TCP/UDP)
- Direction (Inbound/Outbound)
- Priority (Lowest wins)

Example:

```
az network nsg rule create \
—resource-group MyGroup \
—nsg-name MyNSG \
—name AllowHTTP \
—priority 100 \
—direction Inbound \
—access Allow \
—protocol Tcp \
—destination-port-ranges 80
```

Application Security Groups (ASGs)

ASGs simplify NSG rule management by grouping VMs with similar roles. Instead of using IP addresses, rules reference ASGs, enabling dynamic and scalable security policies.

Azure Firewall

A cloud-native, fully managed, stateful firewall with built-in high availability and unrestricted cloud scalability. Features include:

- Threat intelligence filtering
- FQDN filtering
- Centralized policy management

- Integration with Log Analytics

DDoS Protection

Azure DDoS Protection comes in two tiers:

- **Basic**: Automatically enabled for all Azure public IPs.
- **Standard**: Advanced protection for enterprise apps, including telemetry, alerts, and mitigation policies.

This service helps defend against volumetric, protocol, and application layer attacks.

Azure Bastion

A secure and fully managed RDP/SSH access solution for VMs without exposing them to public IPs. All traffic flows through the Azure Portal over HTTPS.

Monitoring and Diagnostics

To operate cloud networks effectively, visibility is paramount. Azure offers rich monitoring tools to observe, analyze, and troubleshoot network performance and availability.

Azure Network Watcher

A suite of diagnostic tools including:

- **Connection Monitor**: Check connectivity between endpoints.

- **IP Flow Verify**: Determine if traffic is allowed or denied.

- **NSG Diagnostics**: View effective NSG rules applied to a VM.

- **Packet Capture**: Capture traffic on a VM for deep analysis.

- **Topology Viewer**: Visualize network structure and dependencies.

Metrics and Logs

Network services in Azure emit **metrics** (quantitative values like bandwidth or latency) and **logs** (descriptive records of events). These can be:

- Viewed in Azure Monitor dashboards

- Analyzed via Log Analytics

- Alerted on using Azure Alerts

Azure Advisor and Network Insights

Azure Advisor provides recommendations for optimizing network performance, security, and cost. Network Insights consolidates this data to help administrators make informed decisions.

Automation and Infrastructure as Code (IaC)

Automating network provisioning is essential for scalability and repeatability. Azure supports multiple IaC tools for networking:

Azure Resource Manager (ARM) Templates

Declarative JSON templates that define Azure resources and their configurations. Ideal for production-grade deployments.

Bicep

A more concise, readable DSL that compiles into ARM templates. Preferred for developers looking to streamline IaC.

Example:

```
resource vnet 'Microsoft.Network/virtualNetworks@2022-01-01' = {

name: 'myVNet'

location: resourceGroup().location

properties: {

addressSpace: {

addressPrefixes: ['10.0.0.0/16']

}

}

}
```

Azure CLI and PowerShell

Azure supports command-line tools for scripting and automating network setup and maintenance.

Terraform

An open-source, cloud-agnostic IaC tool that supports Azure through the azurerm provider. Used extensively for managing complex, multi-cloud environments.

Integration with Other Azure Services

Azure networking is deeply integrated with nearly every other service:

- **Azure Kubernetes Service (AKS)**: Integrated CNI and networking policies
- **Azure App Service**: VNet integration for secure backend access
- **Azure SQL/Storage**: Private Link and service endpoints for secure access
- **Azure DevOps**: Pipelines to deploy and test network infrastructure

Summary

Azure's networking capabilities are vast and highly customizable, designed to accommodate everything from small business websites to enterprise-grade, globally distributed applications. Whether you're connecting a single VM to the internet or building a hybrid mesh with thousands of nodes across regions, Azure provides the tools to do so securely, efficiently, and at scale.

From foundational services like VNets and NSGs to advanced features like Azure Firewall, Front Door, and ExpressRoute, mastering these capabilities empowers architects and administrators to build resilient, high-performance infrastructures tailored to modern digital workloads.

In the next section, we will explore the key terminologies and concepts that underpin Azure networking, providing the vocabulary and conceptual framework needed to confidently navigate and design in the Azure networking space.

Key Terminologies and Concepts

Before diving deeper into Azure networking implementation and design, it is essential to understand the core terminologies and concepts that form the foundation of all networking in Azure. These terms are used consistently throughout the Azure platform and across this book, and understanding them early will make more advanced topics easier to grasp and apply effectively.

This section presents an in-depth exploration of the most important networking-related terms in Azure, complete with explanations, examples, and context around how and why they are used.

Virtual Network (VNet)

A **Virtual Network (VNet)** is Azure's primary network construct. It is a logically isolated network within the Azure environment that allows Azure resources (such as VMs, containers, databases, and web apps) to communicate with one another, with the internet, or with on-premises networks.

A VNet is similar to a traditional on-premises network but with the added benefits of cloud scalability, flexibility, and integration.

Key points:

- Each VNet has a defined IP address space (CIDR block).
- VNets are region-specific.
- Resources within a VNet can communicate without public IP addresses.

Example:

az network vnet create \

—name MyVNet \

—resource-group MyResourceGroup \

—location eastus \

—address-prefix 10.1.0.0/16

Subnet

Subnets are subdivisions of a VNet's IP address space. They allow you to segment a network into smaller, manageable, and secure sections. Resources are deployed within subnets, and you can apply granular security and routing rules at the subnet level.

Benefits of subnetting:

- Logical organization of workloads (e.g., web, application, database tiers).
- Layered security using NSGs per subnet.
- Traffic flow control between tiers.

Example:

az network vnet subnet create \

—address-prefixes 10.1.1.0/24 \

—name WebSubnet \

—vnet-name MyVNet \

—resource-group MyResourceGroup

Network Security Group (NSG)

A **Network Security Group (NSG)** contains a list of security rules that allow or deny network traffic to resources connected to Azure VNets. NSGs can be associated with subnets or individual network interfaces (NICs).

Each rule defines:

- Priority (100–4096, lower value = higher priority)
- Source and destination IPs
- Port range
- Protocol (TCP/UDP)
- Direction (Inbound/Outbound)
- Action (Allow/Deny)

NSGs are a critical component of the **defense-in-depth** strategy.

Example:

az network nsg rule create \

—resource-group MyResourceGroup \

—nsg-name MyNSG \

—name AllowHTTP \

—priority 100 \

—direction Inbound \

—access Allow \

—protocol Tcp \

—destination-port-ranges 80

Public IP Address

Azure resources that require communication with the internet typically use a **Public IP Address**. These can be:

- **Dynamic**: IP assigned at resource creation and may change upon restart.
- **Static**: IP remains the same until explicitly released.

Public IPs can be used for:

- Load balancers
- Virtual machines
- VPN gateways
- Application gateways

Public IPs can be IPv4 or IPv6.

Private IP Address

Private IP Addresses are used for internal communication within a VNet or across peered VNets. These IPs are allocated from the subnet address range and are not routable from the internet.

By default, Azure assigns a dynamic private IP to resources, but you can reserve a static private IP if required.

Use cases:

- Secure communication between backend services
- Internal-only applications
- Database access

Route Table and User-Defined Routes (UDRs)

Azure automatically provides **system routes** that enable traffic flow between subnets, VNets, and the internet. However, when more control is needed, **User-Defined Routes (UDRs)** can be applied.

Use cases:

- Forcing traffic through a firewall or network virtual appliance (NVA)
- Customizing inter-subnet or inter-VNet routing
- Blocking internet-bound traffic

Each route consists of:

- Destination (CIDR block)

- Next hop type (Virtual Appliance, VNet Gateway, etc.)
- Next hop IP address (if using a virtual appliance)

Example:

az network route-table route create \

—resource-group MyResourceGroup \

—route-table-name MyRouteTable \

—name ForceTrafficToFirewall \

—address-prefix 0.0.0.0/0 \

—next-hop-type VirtualAppliance \

—next-hop-ip-address 10.1.1.4

VNet Peering

VNet Peering connects two VNets to allow resources in each to communicate as if they were on the same network. Peering can be:

- **Intra-region (Regional Peering)**: Lower latency and cost
- **Inter-region (Global Peering)**: Enables cross-region connectivity

Peered VNets must not have overlapping address spaces.

Peering is ideal for:

- Large enterprise network architectures

- Multi-tiered applications across VNets
- Inter-departmental network segmentation

Azure DNS and Private DNS Zones

Azure provides DNS services that enable name resolution for Azure resources:

- **Azure DNS**: Public DNS hosting that allows you to manage DNS records for domains hosted in Azure.
- **Private DNS Zones**: Allow internal name resolution within VNets.

You can link Private DNS Zones to VNets to allow seamless communication between services using fully qualified domain names (FQDNs).

Azure Bastion

Azure Bastion provides secure and seamless RDP/SSH connectivity to VMs directly from the Azure portal without exposing them to the public internet. It helps prevent exposure of administrative ports like 22 or 3389.

Key advantages:

- No public IP required for VMs
- Access over TLS via Azure Portal
- Session logging support

Load Balancer

Azure offers Layer 4 load balancing for distributing network traffic across multiple backend resources:

- **Basic Load Balancer**: Intended for development and test workloads.
- **Standard Load Balancer**: Offers higher scalability, availability zones, diagnostics, and more.

It supports:

- Inbound NAT rules
- Health probes
- Session persistence

Use cases:

- Distributing traffic across VMs in a scale set
- Balancing workloads across zones
- Enabling high availability

Application Gateway

The **Azure Application Gateway** is a Layer 7 (HTTP/HTTPS) load balancer that supports application-level routing decisions.

Key features:

- URL-based routing

- Multi-site hosting
- SSL termination
- Web Application Firewall (WAF) integration

Best suited for:

- Web apps requiring intelligent routing
- Scenarios with SSL offloading
- Application layer security enforcement

Azure Front Door

Azure Front Door provides global HTTP/HTTPS load balancing and web acceleration using Microsoft's global edge network.

Key benefits:

- Anycast-based routing
- Application acceleration via caching
- TLS offloading
- Health probes and failover

Use cases:

- Global applications with multi-region backends
- Highly available, low-latency web apps

ExpressRoute

ExpressRoute enables private, dedicated connectivity between your on-premises infrastructure and Azure datacenters.

Characteristics:

- Not routed over the public internet
- Higher reliability and throughput
- Predictable latency
- Available in multiple tiers and metering models

Example use cases:

- Enterprise workloads with strict compliance
- Large data transfers
- Financial services requiring private networks

Virtual Network Gateway

This gateway facilitates VPN-based or ExpressRoute-based connectivity to on-premises networks.

Types:

- **VPN Gateway**: Site-to-site and point-to-site encrypted tunnels.
- **ExpressRoute Gateway**: Connects VNets to ExpressRoute circuits.

Gateway SKUs determine:

- Throughput
- Number of connections
- Features (e.g., BGP support)

Service Endpoints and Private Link

These features secure Azure service traffic:

- **Service Endpoints**: Extend your VNet to Azure services over Microsoft backbone, improving security and performance.
- **Private Link**: Access Azure PaaS services via private IPs within your VNet.

These help eliminate exposure of sensitive services to the public internet.

Azure Firewall

A managed, cloud-native stateful firewall with built-in high availability and scalability.

Features include:

- Application and network rule filtering
- Threat intelligence-based filtering
- Logging and analytics with Azure Monitor

Azure Firewall Premium also supports:

- TLS inspection

- IDPS (Intrusion Detection and Prevention System)
- URL filtering

Network Watcher

Azure Network Watcher offers diagnostic and monitoring capabilities for network infrastructure.

Components:

- **Topology viewer**
- **IP Flow Verify**
- **Packet capture**
- **Connection monitor**

Helps identify:

- Misconfigured NSGs
- Dropped packets
- Latency issues

Summary

These key terminologies form the backbone of Azure's networking platform. Mastering these concepts enables you to:

- Design networks that scale across regions and subscriptions

- Secure your infrastructure against internal and external threats
- Optimize performance and reliability for business-critical applications
- Monitor, diagnose, and troubleshoot with confidence

As you proceed through this book, these terms will be referenced repeatedly in practical configurations, architectural discussions, and troubleshooting scenarios. They are not just definitions—they are the language of cloud networking.

In the next chapter, we'll take a hands-on approach to setting up your first Azure Virtual Network, putting many of these concepts into action with real-world scenarios and configurations.

Chapter 2: Setting Up Your First Azure Virtual Network

Creating a VNet Using the Azure Portal

Creating a Virtual Network (VNet) is often the very first step in deploying resources on Azure. Whether you're setting up a test environment, a production web application, or a hybrid cloud architecture, the VNet provides the foundation upon which everything else is built. While many developers and engineers prefer using Infrastructure as Code (IaC) for repeatability, understanding how to manually configure a VNet using the Azure Portal helps to build foundational knowledge of Azure networking components and relationships.

This section provides a comprehensive, step-by-step walkthrough for creating a Virtual Network using the Azure Portal. It will cover not only the core process but also delve into associated settings like address space, subnets, DNS, and security considerations that need to be thought through at the creation phase.

Planning Your VNet Design

Before launching into the portal, it's important to plan your network topology and address space. Azure uses Classless Inter-Domain Routing (CIDR) notation for IP addressing. Your VNet's address space and subnets should be designed to accommodate current and future scaling needs.

Key considerations:

- Will the network need to connect to on-premises infrastructure?

- How many tiers will your application require (web, app, database)?
- Are there any IP overlaps to avoid with existing networks?
- What address space will you reserve for future use?

Example:

- VNet Address Space: 10.100.0.0/16
  - Subnet1 (Web): 10.100.1.0/24
  - Subnet2 (App): 10.100.2.0/24
  - Subnet3 (DB): 10.100.3.0/24

A /24 subnet provides 256 addresses (254 usable), enough for many workloads.

Step-by-Step: Creating a VNet in Azure Portal

1. **Log into the Azure Portal**

   Navigate to:https://portal.azure.com[1]

2. **Search for Virtual Network**

   In the search bar at the top, type "Virtual Network" and click on the result. Then click **Create.**

3. **Basics Tab**

   Fill out the required information:

1. https://portal.azure.com/

○ **Subscription**: Choose your Azure subscription.

○ **Resource Group**: Either create a new one or use an existing one.

○ **Name**: Enter a name for your VNet (e.g., MyFirstVNet).

○ **Region**: Select the region where you want to deploy this VNet.

4. *Tip*: Choose a region closest to your users or resources for reduced latency.

5. **IP Addresses Tab**

○ **IPv4 Address Space**: Add an address space, e.g., 10.10.0.0/16.

○ **Subnets**:

▪ Add a subnet, e.g., FrontendSubnet with address range 10.10.1.0/24.

▪ Add another subnet if needed, e.g., BackendSubnet with 10.10.2.0/24.

6. *Note*: Do not overlap address spaces across VNets or on-premises networks.

7. **Security Tab**

Decide whether to enable:

○ **Bastion Host**: For secure remote VM access.

○ **Firewall**: Optional; can be configured later.

○ **DDoS Protection**: Standard tier can be enabled here or via Azure Security Center.

8. You can leave these disabled for now unless you have specific needs.

9. **Tags Tab**

Assign tags for cost tracking and organization. Example:

○ Environment : Development

○ Owner : NetworkingTeam

10. **Review + Create**

Review all configurations. If everything looks good, click **Create**.

Azure will now provision your VNet, which may take a few seconds to a minute. Once complete, you can navigate to it from the **Virtual Networks** blade in the portal.

Post-Creation Configuration and Exploration

Once the VNet is created, there are several additional tasks and checks to perform.

Inspecting the VNet

From the VNet overview page, you'll see:

- **Address Space**

- **Subnets**
- **Connected Devices**
- **Peerings**
- **DNS Settings**
- **Security** options like NSGs and firewalls

Adding or Modifying Subnets

You can add new subnets later by clicking **Subnets > + Subnet**. For example, you might add a MonitoringSubnet later with 10.10.4.0/24.

Each subnet can have:

- NSG association
- Route table association
- Service endpoint configurations

Configuring DNS

Navigate to **DNS servers** under the VNet settings:

- Default: Azure-provided DNS.
- Custom: Use internal DNS like Active Directory or third-party providers.

Example:

- Custom DNS IP: 10.10.4.4 (your internal DNS server)

This ensures name resolution works properly across hybrid environments.

Adding Network Security Groups (NSGs)

While NSGs are not created automatically during VNet creation, they are essential for controlling traffic.

Steps:

1. Create a new NSG from the **Network Security Groups** blade.
2. Add inbound and outbound rules.
3. Associate the NSG with the subnet (or individual NICs).

Example Rule:

- Allow TCP on port 80 and 443 for HTTP/HTTPS web access.

- Deny all inbound traffic by default.

Associating Route Tables

If you need custom routing, create a **Route Table** and assign it to one or more subnets.

Example use case:

- Directing all traffic through a firewall at 10.10.0.4.

Route Table > + Route:

- Address prefix: 0.0.0.0/0
- Next hop type: Virtual Appliance
- Next hop address: 10.10.0.4

Then associate the route table with a subnet in your VNet.

Integrating Azure Resources into the VNet

Once the VNet is created, you can start deploying other Azure resources into it:

- **Virtual Machines**: Ensure they are placed into the correct subnet and associated with relevant NSGs.
- **App Services**: Use **VNet integration** to connect to backend services.
- **Databases**: Use **Private Endpoints** or **Service Endpoints** to access PaaS databases securely.

Azure resources with virtual networking support typically have a **Networking** tab during creation that allows you to select a VNet and subnet.

Common Mistakes to Avoid

- **Overlapping IP Address Spaces**: Especially problematic in hybrid setups.
- **Skipping NSG Configuration**: Leads to unnecessary exposure or blocked traffic.

- **Placing All Resources in One Subnet**: Reduces manageability and control.

- **Ignoring DNS Settings**: Causes service discovery failures in hybrid and microservice environments.

Best Practices

- Use **CIDR ranges that avoid conflict** with on-premises networks (e.g., avoid 192.168.0.0/16).

- Reserve **IP ranges for future subnets** and growth.

- Apply **NSGs to subnets** for layered security rather than individual NICs when possible.

- Leverage **tags** for environment, cost center, and ownership tracking.

- Start simple but **design for scale**—you can always evolve your network.

Summary

Creating a Virtual Network using the Azure Portal is a straightforward process, but it requires thoughtful planning to ensure long-term scalability and security. Understanding the implications of address space, subnetting, DNS, and network security is key to building a robust Azure environment. The portal provides a user-friendly interface for beginners while still offering the depth needed by experienced architects.

In the next section, we'll explore how to define address spaces and segment networks with subnets to implement well-structured, scalable virtual environments that support enterprise-grade applications.

Address Spaces, Subnets, and Network Segmentation

Proper planning of address spaces and subnets is critical to building a scalable, secure, and manageable Azure network. Whether you're deploying a small development environment or a complex enterprise application spanning multiple regions, defining clear IP addressing and segmentation policies lays the foundation for stability and future growth. In this section, we'll examine how to effectively structure your virtual network using address spaces and subnets and implement network segmentation strategies that align with modern architectural and security best practices.

Understanding Address Spaces in Azure VNets

Every Azure Virtual Network (VNet) requires one or more **IPv4 address spaces**, defined using CIDR (Classless Inter-Domain Routing) notation. This address space is the pool from which subnets derive their IP ranges.

Example of a VNet address space:

- 10.0.0.0/16 – Provides 65,536 IP addresses (256 × /24 subnets)

You can also define **multiple address spaces** within a single VNet. This is useful in scenarios where:

- You're integrating two pre-existing IP schemes.

- A portion of your address space becomes exhausted and needs expansion.
- You are peering multiple VNets and need to avoid overlap.

Best Practices for Address Spaces

- Avoid overlapping address ranges between VNets, especially when planning for VNet peering or VPN connectivity.
- Choose ranges that won't conflict with on-premises networks.
- Reserve large enough spaces for future subnets and growth.
- Use private IP address ranges from RFC 1918:
  - 10.0.0.0/8
  - 172.16.0.0/12
  - 192.168.0.0/16

Creating and Managing Subnets

Subnets are logical subdivisions of a VNet's address space. They are used to:

- Isolate resources by function or security level (e.g., web, app, DB).
- Apply different security policies and route tables.

- Delegate subnet IPs to services like Azure Bastion or Azure Firewall.

A subnet is defined by its own CIDR block, which must be a non-overlapping subset of the VNet's address space.

Example:

- VNet Address Space: 10.0.0.0/16
  - Web Subnet: 10.0.1.0/24
  - App Subnet: 10.0.2.0/24
  - DB Subnet: 10.0.3.0/24

Each /24 subnet provides 256 addresses, though only 251 are usable due to reserved addresses.

Reserved IPs in each subnet:

- First IP: Network address
- Last IP: Broadcast address
- 3 additional Azure-reserved IPs

Creating Subnets via Azure Portal

1. Navigate to your Virtual Network in the Azure Portal.
2. Under **Settings**, select **Subnets**.
3. Click **+ Subnet**.
4. Enter:

- ○ **Name**: E.g., AppSubnet
- ○ **Address Range**: E.g., 10.0.2.0/24
- ○ Associate NSG and Route Table if needed.

5. Click **Save.**

Creating Subnets via CLI

az network vnet subnet create \

—resource-group MyResourceGroup \

—vnet-name MyVNet \

—name AppSubnet \

—address-prefix 10.0.2.0/24

Subnet Delegation

Azure allows you to delegate an entire subnet to a specific Azure service, such as:

- Azure Kubernetes Service (AKS)
- Azure Container Instances
- Azure Bastion
- Application Gateway

This is required when those services need to manage the subnet internally.

Example:

```
az network vnet subnet update \
—name AksSubnet \
—vnet-name MyVNet \
—resource-group MyResourceGroup \
—delegations Microsoft.ContainerService/managedClusters
```

Delegation ensures proper IP allocation and avoids deployment issues.

Implementing Network Segmentation

Network segmentation is the practice of dividing a network into multiple smaller parts (segments) to:

- Enhance security by isolating resources.
- Improve performance and manageability.
- Apply different policies based on business needs.

In Azure, segmentation is primarily achieved through:

- Subnets
- NSGs (Network Security Groups)
- Route tables
- Peering and hub-spoke models

Segmentation by Function

This is the most common model where each tier or function of your architecture resides in its own subnet.

Example:

- WebTierSubnet – open to HTTP/S traffic
- AppTierSubnet – only accessible from WebTierSubnet
- DataTierSubnet – restricted to AppTierSubnet access only

Segmentation by Environment

Different environments (Dev, Test, Prod) can use different subnets, VNets, or even subscriptions.

Benefits:

- Reduces the risk of changes in dev affecting production.
- Enables separate policies and monitoring.
- Eases compliance audits.

Segmentation by Trust Level

Using the **zero trust** model, networks are segmented based on risk and trust.

Example:

- Internal subnet for backend services

- DMZ subnet for public-facing web apps
- Admin subnet for management access

Each subnet would have strict NSG rules controlling ingress and egress.

Designing for Scalability

When planning your address spaces and subnets, consider:

- **Growth**: Use CIDR ranges that allow for future subdivisions. For example, a /16 VNet can contain 256 /24 subnets.
- **Isolation**: Each service or application component should be isolated for easier security management.
- **Automation**: Define subnets and address ranges in templates for consistent deployments.

Common Design Patterns

Flat Network

- Single VNet and single large subnet
- Simple but not scalable or secure
- Suitable only for testing environments

Tiered Network

- Three subnets (Web, App, DB)

- NSGs and route tables used for control
- Widely used in production workloads

Hub-and-Spoke

- Centralized hub with shared services (e.g., DNS, firewall)
- Spoke VNets for apps or teams
- Uses VNet peering for connectivity

Multi-Region Network

- VNets deployed in multiple regions
- Peering or VPN gateways for connectivity
- Supports global redundancy and compliance

Example Design Scenario

Let's design a small three-tier application network:

1. VNet Address Space: 10.20.0.0/16
2. Subnets:

  - WebSubnet: 10.20.1.0/24
  - AppSubnet: 10.20.2.0/24
  - DbSubnet: 10.20.3.0/24

NSG Rules:

- WebSubnet allows inbound HTTP/HTTPS from Internet
- AppSubnet allows traffic from WebSubnet only
- DbSubnet allows traffic from AppSubnet only

Routing:

- Use default system routing unless custom inspection (firewall) is needed.

Benefits:

- Clear separation of responsibilities.
- Easier to apply least privilege access.
- Simplifies troubleshooting and compliance checks.

IP Exhaustion and Planning Ahead

Always plan for:

- IP address exhaustion (keep spare address ranges)
- Expansion (leave gaps between subnets)
- Service integration (some services require dedicated IPs/subnets)

Azure recommends not using all available IPs in a subnet to allow for scaling and service requirements.

Summary

Subnets and address spaces are not just configuration steps—they are strategic tools for shaping your Azure environment. They impact security, availability, scalability, and performance. By carefully defining IP ranges, segmenting traffic with subnets, and applying the principles of isolation and delegation, you create a solid foundation for anything you build in the cloud.

The next section will focus on **Network Security Groups (NSGs)** and show how they are applied to subnets and individual resources to enforce fine-grained access control across your virtual network.

Configuring Network Security Groups (NSGs)

A well-designed network is not only about connectivity—it is also about **control**. Azure's **Network Security Groups (NSGs)** play a central role in securing your virtual networks by allowing or denying traffic based on rules that you define. NSGs act as stateful, distributed firewalls and are essential for enforcing a layered security strategy across your Azure resources.

In this section, you'll learn what NSGs are, how they work, how to create and apply them to subnets and individual network interfaces, and how they integrate with Azure's broader security and monitoring tools. You'll also see practical examples and best practices that help maintain control over traffic without creating unmanageable rule sets.

What Is a Network Security Group?

A **Network Security Group (NSG)** is a security boundary that contains **rules** used to filter inbound and outbound network traffic. NSGs can be applied to:

- **Subnets**: Rules apply to all resources within the subnet.
- **Network Interface Cards (NICs)**: Rules apply to a specific VM or service instance.

Each NSG can contain up to:

- 1000 rules per NSG (default limit)
- Separate sets of **inbound** and **outbound** rules

Rules are processed in order of **priority**, where a lower number has higher precedence.

Key Rule Properties

Each rule includes the following parameters:

- **Name**: Unique identifier for the rule.
- **Priority**: Integer between 100 and 4096. Lower = evaluated earlier.
- **Direction**: Inbound or Outbound.
- **Access**: Allow or Deny.
- **Protocol**: TCP, UDP, or * (any).

- **Source/Destination**: IP address, range, or tag (e.g., Internet, VirtualNetwork).

- **Port Ranges**: One or more ports (e.g., 80, 443, 1000–2000).

NSGs are **stateful**, which means if you allow inbound traffic, the corresponding outbound reply is automatically allowed.

Default Rules

Every NSG comes with **three default inbound and outbound rules**, which cannot be removed but can be overridden by higher-priority rules.

Default Inbound Rules:

1. Allow VNet Inbound
2. Allow Azure Load Balancer Inbound
3. Deny All Inbound

Default Outbound Rules:

1. Allow VNet Outbound
2. Allow Internet Outbound
3. Deny All Outbound

Creating an NSG Using Azure Portal

1. In the Azure Portal, search for **Network Security Groups**.

2. Click + **Create**.

3. Choose:

- Resource Group
- Region
- NSG Name (e.g., WebTierNSG)

4. Click **Review + Create**, then **Create**.

Once created, open the NSG to start adding rules.

Adding Inbound Rules

Example: Allow HTTP and HTTPS traffic to a web server.

1. Go to your NSG > **Inbound security rules** > **+ Add.**
2. Rule Name: AllowHTTP
3. Priority: 100
4. Source: Any
5. Destination: Any
6. Destination Port Ranges: 80
7. Protocol: TCP
8. Action: Allow
9. Repeat for port 443 (HTTPS)

This allows public web traffic to reach resources protected by this NSG.

Assigning NSG to a Subnet

1. Navigate to your Virtual Network.
2. Select **Subnets** > choose the desired subnet.
3. Under **Network Security Group**, select your NSG.
4. Click **Save**.

This attaches the NSG to the subnet, applying all rules to any resources within.

Assigning NSG to a NIC

1. Go to the target Virtual Machine.
2. Under **Networking**, select the **NIC**.
3. Click **Network security group** > **Associate**.
4. Choose your NSG and click **Save**.

Use NIC-level NSGs for fine-grained control of specific VMs or applications.

Creating NSG via CLI

```
# Create NSG

az network nsg create \

—resource-group MyResourceGroup \

—name WebTierNSG \

—location eastus

# Add inbound rule for port 80

az network nsg rule create \

—resource-group MyResourceGroup \

—nsg-name WebTierNSG \

—name AllowHTTP \

—priority 100 \
```

—direction Inbound \

—access Allow \

—protocol Tcp \

—destination-port-range 80 \

—source-address-prefix '*' \

—destination-address-prefix '*'

Using Application Security Groups (ASGs)

Application Security Groups (ASGs) allow you to group VMs logically and apply NSG rules based on group membership instead of IPs.

Example:

- Create ASG: WebServers
- Assign to VMs in the web tier
- Create NSG rule that allows inbound HTTP to ASG WebServers

Benefits:

- Simplifies rule management
- Automatically adjusts as resources scale

az network asg create \

—resource-group MyResourceGroup \

—name WebServers

Then assign the ASG to the NIC of a VM via the Portal or CLI.

Scenario: Three-Tier Application with NSGs

Assume you have three subnets:

- WebSubnet
- AppSubnet
- DBSubnet

NSG: WebNSG

- Allow Inbound HTTP/HTTPS from Internet
- Deny all other inbound
- Allow all outbound

NSG: AppNSG

- Allow Inbound from WebSubnet (port 5000)
- Deny all other inbound
- Allow Outbound to DBSubnet (port 1433)

NSG: DBNSG

- Allow Inbound from AppSubnet (port 1433)
- Deny all other inbound

- Deny all outbound except to logging services

This design enforces **least privilege** and protects each layer of the application independently.

Monitoring and Troubleshooting NSGs

Azure provides tools to help monitor and debug NSG configurations:

NSG Flow Logs

Enable flow logs for an NSG to capture information about allowed/denied flows:

- Source and destination IP/port
- Direction
- Action
- Protocol

Stored in Azure Storage or sent to Log Analytics for querying.

```
az network watcher flow-log configure \
—resource-group MyResourceGroup \
—nsg WebTierNSG \
—enabled true \
—retention 7 \
—storage-account mystorageaccount
```

IP Flow Verify

Use Network Watcher's **IP Flow Verify** to check if traffic is allowed or denied between two endpoints based on NSG rules.

Effective Security Rules

For any NIC, you can view **Effective Security Rules** in the Azure Portal to understand which NSG rules are applied and why.

Best Practices for NSG Configuration

- **Use ASGs** instead of hardcoding IPs in NSG rules.
- **Separate NSGs per tier or function** to maintain clarity.
- **Log and monitor** NSG flows to validate policies and detect anomalies.
- **Avoid overlapping rules** with conflicting priorities.
- **Tag and document** each rule to identify its purpose.
- Apply **deny-all-by-default**, then allow only what is necessary.
- Prefer **subnet-level NSGs** for broad policies, and NIC-level for exceptions.

NSGs and Integration with Azure Services

Many Azure services interact with NSGs:

- **Azure Load Balancer**: Requires rules to allow health probes and frontend IPs.
- **Azure Bastion**: Requires specific ports to be allowed between user and VM.
- **Virtual Machine Scale Sets**: Use ASGs and NSGs to simplify management at scale.
- **Private Link Services**: Ensure correct NSG rules for inbound private traffic.

Always consult Azure documentation for service-specific networking requirements.

Summary

Network Security Groups are a powerful tool in your Azure security arsenal. They offer flexible, granular, and scalable control over traffic flow at both the subnet and VM level. With proper use of NSGs, ASGs, and flow logs, you can enforce enterprise-grade security policies while still maintaining agility and ease of deployment. Mastering NSG configuration is critical for any Azure networking professional, and it's one of the first areas auditors and security teams will examine when assessing your cloud environment.

In the next section, we'll expand this foundation by introducing **Route Tables and User-Defined Routes (UDRs)**, which enable you to control the flow of network traffic across your Azure infrastructure.

Implementing Route Tables and User-Defined Routes

When working with cloud networks, particularly in complex or hybrid environments, it becomes crucial to control the flow of traffic within and between networks. In Azure, this control is provided through **Route Tables** and **User-Defined Routes (UDRs)**. While Azure automatically creates system routes to enable basic connectivity, real-world applications often demand a higher level of customization—routing traffic through firewalls, virtual appliances, or forcing specific network paths.

This section covers the fundamentals of Azure routing, introduces route tables and user-defined routes, and walks through advanced routing scenarios. You'll learn how to configure and apply custom routes to subnets, how to route traffic through network appliances, and how to troubleshoot and validate route behavior in a live Azure environment.

Understanding Azure Routing

Every Virtual Network (VNet) in Azure automatically includes a system-generated set of **default routes**. These routes facilitate traffic between resources in the same VNet, to the internet, and to any connected peered VNets or gateways.

Default system routes include:

Source	Destination	Next Hop Type
Default	VNet	Virtual Network
Default	Internet	Internet
Default	0.0.0.0/0	Internet
Default	10.0.0.0/8, 172.16.0.0/12, 192.168.0.0/16	None (local)

These default routes may be sufficient for simple scenarios, but in enterprise-grade solutions, administrators often need to override them for custom routing needs.

What Are Route Tables?

A **Route Table** in Azure is a collection of custom routes that can be associated with one or more subnets. These tables can override the default system routes for traffic leaving the subnet.

Route tables are composed of **User-Defined Routes (UDRs)**. Each route has the following components:

- **Address Prefix**: The destination IP address range.
- **Next Hop Type**:
  - Virtual Appliance (e.g., firewall or NVA)
  - Virtual Network Gateway
  - Internet
  - VNet Peering
  - None

- **Next Hop IP Address**: Required for certain next hop types (e.g., Virtual Appliance).

Creating a Route Table (Portal)

1. Navigate to **Route tables** in the Azure Portal.
2. Click + **Create.**
3. Enter the **Name, Region**, and **Resource Group**.
4. Click **Review + Create**, then **Create**.

After the route table is created, go to it and:

- Click **Routes** > + **Add.**

- Enter route details.

Example:

- Name: RouteToFirewall

- Address prefix: 0.0.0.0/0

- Next hop type: Virtual Appliance

- Next hop IP address: 10.0.1.4

This will send all outbound traffic to the appliance at 10.0.1.4.

Creating a Route Table via CLI

Create the route table

az network route-table create \

—name MyRouteTable \

—resource-group MyResourceGroup \

—location eastus

Add a route to send all traffic to a firewall

az network route-table route create \

—resource-group MyResourceGroup \

—route-table-name MyRouteTable \

—name DefaultToFirewall \

—address-prefix 0.0.0.0/0 \

—next-hop-type VirtualAppliance \

—next-hop-ip-address 10.0.0.4

Associating a Route Table with a Subnet

A route table must be explicitly associated with a **subnet** to become active.

Azure Portal:

- Go to the target VNet > Subnets.
- Select the subnet.
- Under **Route table**, select your custom route table.
- Save.

Azure CLI:

az network vnet subnet update \

—resource-group MyResourceGroup \

—vnet-name MyVNet \

—name WebSubnet \

—route-table MyRouteTable

Example Scenario: Forcing Traffic Through a Firewall

Assume your network topology:

- VNet: 10.0.0.0/16
- Subnet1 (Web): 10.0.1.0/24
- Subnet2 (Firewall): 10.0.2.0/24
- Azure Firewall IP: 10.0.2.4

You want all internet-bound traffic from WebSubnet to pass through Azure Firewall. You would:

1. Create a route table with a route:
   - Prefix: 0.0.0.0/0
   - Next hop: Virtual Appliance
   - IP: 10.0.2.4
2. Associate this route table with the WebSubnet.

Now, any traffic from WebSubnet to the internet will go through the firewall at 10.0.2.4.

Advanced Routing Scenarios

Routing Between VNets with NVAs

When you peer two VNets and place a Network Virtual Appliance (NVA) in the hub, you can route all spoke traffic through the hub by creating custom routes that point to the NVA as the next hop.

For example:

- Spoke VNet address space: 10.1.0.0/16
- Hub NVA IP: 10.0.0.4

In each spoke subnet's route table:

- Add route: 0.0.0.0/0 → Virtual Appliance (10.0.0.4)

Isolating Subnets

You can prevent communication between subnets in the same VNet using UDRs.

For example:

- Add a route in AppSubnet: 10.0.3.0/24 → None
- This drops traffic bound for the database subnet.

Use this in conjunction with NSGs for an extra layer of protection.

Forced Tunneling

Forced tunneling routes all internet-bound traffic to an on-premises edge device via a VPN gateway. This is used in scenarios requiring central inspection or logging.

Steps:

1. Create a route: 0.0.0.0/0 → Virtual Network Gateway
2. Apply it to the relevant subnets.
3. Ensure the on-premises device is configured to accept and forward traffic appropriately.

Note: Be cautious—misconfiguring forced tunneling can result in loss of internet access.

Validating and Troubleshooting Routes

Azure provides tools to view and debug effective routing paths.

Effective Routes

1. Go to the VM > Networking > NIC.
2. Click **Effective Routes**.

You'll see a list of all active routes, including:

- System routes
- UDRs
- BGP routes (if using ExpressRoute or VPN)

This tool helps validate whether your UDRs are taking effect.

Network Watcher – IP Flow Verify

Use this tool to determine if a packet is allowed or denied based on NSGs and UDRs.

Example:

- Source IP: 10.0.1.10
- Destination IP: 8.8.8.8
- Port: 443
- Protocol: TCP

It will return **Allowed** or **Denied** with reasoning.

Packet Captures

Using Network Watcher, you can perform packet captures on VMs to:

- Inspect traffic paths
- Validate whether packets are routed through the desired device
- Confirm latency or packet loss issues

Best Practices for Route Tables and UDRs

- **Minimize the number of route tables** unless isolation or control is needed.

- Use **next hop Virtual Appliance** for service chaining (firewalls, proxies).
- Avoid overlapping or conflicting routes.
- Combine **NSGs and UDRs** for maximum traffic control.
- Always test UDRs in non-production before applying broadly.
- Document all routes with naming conventions and tags.
- **Monitor route effectiveness** using Azure tools like Effective Routes.

Common Pitfalls

- Assigning incorrect next hop IPs (e.g., IP not in same subnet).
- Forgetting to associate route tables to subnets.
- Creating circular routes with peering and transit networks.
- Overwriting system routes unintentionally, breaking basic connectivity.

Summary

Custom routing in Azure using Route Tables and User-Defined Routes gives you precise control over how traffic flows across your virtual network infrastructure. Whether you're implementing a hub-and-spoke topology, forcing traffic through a firewall, or isolating subnets for security, UDRs empower you to shape traffic flows to meet both operational and compliance requirements. Combined with effective monitoring and NSGs, they form a powerful toolset for designing secure, resilient, and manageable cloud network architectures.

In the next chapter, we will explore **Inter-VNet Communication**, beginning with VNet Peering and its role in connecting distributed workloads across regions and network boundaries.

Chapter 3: Inter-VNet Communication

VNet Peering: Concepts and Setup

Azure Virtual Network (VNet) peering enables direct network connectivity between two or more VNets within the same Azure region or across regions. It is a foundational concept for building scalable, secure, and high-performance network architectures in the cloud. Peering allows VNets to communicate as if they were part of the same network, without requiring additional gateways, VPNs, or public internet exposure.

Conceptual Overview of VNet Peering

VNet peering establishes a low-latency, high-bandwidth connection between VNets. Once peered, resources in each VNet can communicate with each other using private IP addresses, much like they would within the same subnet.

Peering connections are non-transitive, meaning if VNet A is peered with VNet B, and VNet B is peered with VNet C, VNet A cannot automatically communicate with VNet C. To establish communication between A and C, a direct peering must also exist between them.

Azure supports two primary types of peering:

- **Regional VNet Peering:** This occurs between VNets in the same Azure region.
- **Global VNet Peering:** This occurs between VNets in different Azure regions.

Benefits of VNet Peering

1. **Low Latency, High Bandwidth:** Communication over the Azure backbone ensures optimal performance.
2. **Private Connectivity:** Traffic does not traverse the public internet, maintaining security and compliance.
3. **No Bandwidth Restrictions:** There are no constraints on the bandwidth of the peering link itself.
4. **Seamless Resource Sharing:** Enables services like Azure SQL Database, App Services, and VMs to interact across VNets.

When to Use VNet Peering

VNet peering is ideal when:

- You need to connect development and production environments.
- Your network design involves a hub-and-spoke topology.
- You are deploying applications that span multiple VNets for isolation or scaling purposes.
- You are working with a multi-region architecture.

Key Considerations

Before implementing VNet peering, it's essential to be aware of the following:

- **IP Address Overlap:** The address spaces of the VNets must not overlap.

- **Transitivity:** Peering is non-transitive. Explicit peerings are required between each pair of VNets that need to communicate.

- **Permissions:** Appropriate Azure RBAC permissions (like Network Contributor) are needed to configure peering.

- **Billing:** Traffic across peered VNets is billed. Same-region peering is cheaper than global peering.

Setting Up VNet Peering Using the Azure Portal

Here's how to peer two VNets (VNetA and VNetB) using the Azure Portal:

1. **Navigate to VNetA:**

○ Open the Azure portal.

○ Go to **Virtual networks** and select **VNetA**.

2. **Initiate Peering:**

○ Under **Settings**, click on **Peerings**.

○ Click + **Add** to create a new peering.

○ Provide a name for the peering from VNetA to VNetB.

○ Choose **Peering link name for remote network**.

○ Under **Virtual network deployment model**, choose **Resource Manager**.

○ For the **Subscription**, select the correct one.

- ○ Select **VNetB** from the **Virtual network** dropdown.
- ○ Enable traffic flow as needed:
  - ▪ Allow traffic from VNetA to VNetB.
  - ▪ Allow traffic from VNetB to VNetA.

3. **Review and Create:**

- ○ Review your settings and click **OK** to create the peering.
- ○ Repeat the process from VNetB if required (mutual peering is optional if bidirectional traffic was enabled in the first step).

Setting Up VNet Peering Using Azure CLI

Azure CLI provides a fast, repeatable way to configure peering. Here's an example:

Variables

VNET_A_NAME="VNetA"

VNET_B_NAME="VNetB"

RESOURCE_GROUP="MyResourceGroup"

Get VNet IDs

VNET_A_ID=$(az network vnet show—resource-group $RESOURCE_GROUP—name $VNET_A_NAME—query id—output tsv)

VNET_B_ID=$(az network vnet show—resource-group $RESOURCE_GROUP—name $VNET_B_NAME—query id—output tsv)

Create peering from A to B

az network vnet peering create \

—name VNetAtoVNetB \

—resource-group $RESOURCE_GROUP \

—vnet-name $VNET_A_NAME \

—remote-vnet $VNET_B_ID \

—allow-vnet-access

Create peering from B to A

az network vnet peering create \

—name VNetBtoVNetA \

—resource-group $RESOURCE_GROUP \

—vnet-name $VNET_B_NAME \

—remote-vnet $VNET_A_ID \

—allow-vnet-access

This script enables full bidirectional peering between the two VNets.

Common Use Cases in Real Environments

Hub-and-Spoke Architectures

In a typical hub-and-spoke model:

- The **hub VNet** contains shared services like firewalls, DNS servers, and Azure Bastion.
- **Spoke VNets** are used for workloads in separate business units or applications.

Each spoke VNet peers with the hub VNet, allowing centralized access to shared services. However, spoke-to-spoke communication requires either direct peering or a transit mechanism (such as a firewall or routing appliance in the hub).

Multi-Region Deployments

When deploying across multiple regions for redundancy and latency optimization, global VNet peering is used to ensure that VNets in different regions can communicate. This is critical for distributed applications and DR (disaster recovery) setups.

Troubleshooting Peering Issues

Issue 1: VNets not communicating

- Ensure both VNets are peered properly.
- Verify that NSG rules are not blocking traffic.
- Check that IP address spaces do not overlap.

Issue 2: One-way communication

- Review the peering settings to ensure bidirectional access is enabled.

- Inspect custom route tables that might be interfering with traffic.

Issue 3: Performance Degradation

- Confirm that traffic is traversing over the Azure backbone and not being forced through a gateway or public endpoint.

- Use **Network Watcher** to analyze latency and throughput.

Best Practices

- **Avoid Overlapping IP Ranges:** Use planned IP addressing to prevent conflicts.

- **Name Peerings Clearly:** Include source and destination in peering names for clarity (e.g., ProdToDevPeering).

- **Use Tags:** Tag your peerings and VNets to facilitate management and cost tracking.

- **Audit Regularly:** Use Azure Policy and diagnostic logs to audit VNet peering configurations.

- **Use Automation:** Where possible, define peering as part of infrastructure-as-code templates to maintain consistency across environments.

Summary

VNet peering is a fundamental building block for scalable and secure network designs in Azure. Whether connecting workloads across development environments, enabling multi-region availability, or implementing advanced topologies like hub-and-spoke, VNet peering offers a simple and cost-effective solution. With the right planning and configuration, you can achieve high availability, optimal performance, and seamless communication across your Azure VNets.

Regional vs. Global Peering

Azure VNet peering supports two primary types of connections—**Regional Peering** and **Global Peering**. While both allow virtual networks to communicate with each other through private IP addresses using the Azure backbone infrastructure, the differences between the two modes are critical in determining performance, cost, and security architecture. Understanding the distinction and appropriate application of each is essential for designing effective network topologies in Azure.

Understanding Regional Peering

Regional VNet peering connects virtual networks within the same Azure region. This is the most straightforward and cost-effective form of VNet peering. When two VNets reside in the same region, traffic between them remains local to the Azure datacenter, leading to minimal latency and cost.

Characteristics of Regional Peering

- **Same Region**: VNets must be in the same Azure region (e.g., East US).
- **High Speed, Low Latency**: Offers near-LAN speeds due to Azure's internal datacenter networking.
- **Least Expensive Option**: Lower data transfer costs compared to global peering.
- **No Bandwidth Bottlenecks**: Communication occurs over Azure's high-speed backbone, without throttling.

Use Cases for Regional Peering

- Connecting frontend and backend tiers in the same region.
- Creating hub-and-spoke networks where all VNets are located in one region.
- Isolating workloads (e.g., dev, test, prod) while still allowing internal communication.

Example: Regional Peering via Azure CLI

```
az network vnet peering create \
—name SpokeToHub \
—resource-group MyResourceGroup \
—vnet-name SpokeVNet \
```

—remote-vnet /subscriptions/<sub-id>/resourceGroups/ MyResourceGroup/providers/Microsoft.Network/ virtualNetworks/HubVNet \

—allow-vnet-access

This command connects SpokeVNet to HubVNet, both within the same region.

Understanding Global Peering

Global VNet peering enables connectivity between VNets located in **different Azure regions**. It is ideal for businesses that require high availability, global reach, and redundancy in their applications.

Characteristics of Global Peering

- **Cross-Region Communication**: VNets can reside in any Azure-supported region.
- **Private Backbone Communication**: Like regional peering, traffic never traverses the public internet.
- **Higher Cost**: Typically incurs higher data transfer charges compared to regional peering.
- **Latency Considerations**: While still low-latency, it's subject to greater physical distance between regions.

Use Cases for Global Peering

- Multi-region deployments to support geographic failover and disaster recovery.

- Global SaaS or PaaS services that need to centralize shared services like identity or logging.
- Regulatory or compliance-driven architectures requiring resource separation across geographies.

Example: Global Peering via PowerShell

```
New-AzVirtualNetworkPeering `

-Name "EastToWestPeering" `

-VirtualNetwork $vnetEast `

-RemoteVirtualNetworkId $vnetWest.Id `

-AllowVirtualNetworkAccess $true
```

This PowerShell snippet peers two VNets in different regions (East US and West US), enabling global communication over the Azure backbone.

Feature Comparison: Regional vs. Global Peering

Feature	**Regional Peering**	**Global Peering**
Geographic Scope	Same region	Different regions
Cost	Lower	Higher
Latency	Very low	Low to moderate
Bandwidth Constraints	None	None
Gateway Requirement	Not required	Not required
Supports Transitive Routing	No	No
Cross-Subscription Support	Yes	Yes
Traffic Over Azure Backbone	Yes	Yes
Allowed for Production Architectures	Yes	Yes

Security and Compliance Considerations

Both regional and global peering use Azure's private network backbone. However, depending on organizational policies, compliance frameworks, and regional regulations (such as GDPR or HIPAA), global peering may require deeper evaluation.

- **Data Residency Laws**: Some jurisdictions may limit cross-border data transfers.

- **Audit Trails**: Use Network Watcher and diagnostic settings to log and audit traffic for compliance purposes.

- **NSGs and Route Tables**: Even though the peering is private, appropriate NSG and UDR configurations are necessary to control traffic between regions.

Performance Factors

Latency

- **Regional Peering**: Sub-millisecond latency is typical. Azure internally optimizes paths within a region.
- **Global Peering**: Depends on physical distance and Azure's regional edge presence. For example, peering between East US and West Europe introduces higher latency compared to peering within West Europe.

Throughput

- Throughput in both peering types is only limited by VM and NIC capabilities, not by the peering itself.

Use the following command to measure latency and packet loss between peered VNets:

az network watcher flow-log show—resource-group MyResourceGroup—nsg-name MyNSG

Cost Implications

Azure charges for data transfer in both regional and global peering, but at different rates:

- **Regional Peering**: Inbound and outbound data are usually less expensive.
- **Global Peering**: Charged per GB of data transferred in both directions, with a higher rate.

To monitor and manage costs, use:

az costmanagement query usage—scope /subscriptions/<sub-id>

Or configure Azure Budgets with alerts to notify when peering costs approach thresholds.

Designing with Peering in Mind

When planning VNet architecture:

1. **Start with Regional Peering**: If your workloads are local to a region, leverage the simplicity and cost-efficiency of regional peering.
2. **Scale to Global Peering**: Introduce global peering when business requirements demand it (e.g., DR, latency optimization for global users).
3. **Implement Hub-and-Spoke Globally**: Create regional hubs, and use global peering to interconnect them while keeping spoke VNets local.
4. **Control Traffic with NSGs and Firewalls**: Peering alone does not provide granular access control; layer in NSGs and Azure Firewall for enterprise control.

Sample Scenario: Multi-Region Web Application

Imagine an organization running a web application with the following architecture:

- Frontend hosted in East US
- Backend and database in West US
- Logging and monitoring centralized in Central US

To enable communication across components, global peering is used:

- East US VNet ⇄ Central US VNet
- West US VNet ⇄ Central US VNet
- Optional peering between East US VNet and West US VNet if direct frontend-backend communication is needed

Using this topology ensures:

- Regional redundancy
- Optimized latency per user base
- Compliance with Azure zone-based availability

Monitoring and Troubleshooting Peering Performance

Use Azure Network Watcher to monitor traffic and performance between peered VNets:

```
az network watcher connection-monitor create \

—name PeeringMonitor \

—resource-group MyResourceGroup \

—location eastus \

—source-resource /subscriptions/<sub-id>/resourceGroups/MyResourceGroup/providers/Microsoft.Network/networkInterfaces/nic-1 \

—dest-address 10.1.0.4 \
```

—protocol Tcp \

—port 80

This helps measure availability and latency of connections across peered networks.

Conclusion

Regional and global VNet peering are core components of scalable, resilient, and secure cloud networking strategies. Regional peering is optimal for localized workloads and offers the best performance at the lowest cost. Global peering, while slightly more expensive, unlocks powerful capabilities for cross-region architectures and redundancy.

Choosing between them—or combining both—depends on your application's geography, performance needs, and compliance landscape. By thoughtfully implementing peering and monitoring it actively, you can ensure your network fabric in Azure is robust, secure, and future-proof.

Cost Implications and Performance Considerations

As organizations scale their Azure network infrastructure, understanding the **cost** and **performance trade-offs** associated with inter-VNet communication—particularly through VNet peering—is critical. Whether deploying applications across multiple VNets in a region, implementing global architectures for disaster recovery, or designing highly available microservices ecosystems, the architectural choices you make can significantly impact your Azure billing and application responsiveness.

This section dives deep into the **cost models, performance metrics**, and **optimization strategies** associated with VNet peering, helping you strike the right balance between performance and cost efficiency.

Overview of Azure VNet Peering Cost Model

Azure VNet peering is not free, but it is **often more economical than using VPN Gateways or ExpressRoute** for internal traffic. Azure charges for both **ingress (incoming)** and **egress (outgoing)** data when using peering, with variations based on whether you're using **regional** or **global peering.**

Cost Model Breakdown

1. **Regional Peering:**

   ○ **Ingress:** Free

   ○ **Egress:** Low cost (varies by region)

   ○ **Billing granularity:** Per GB

2. **Global Peering:**

   ○ **Ingress and Egress:** Both charged

   ○ **Higher rate per GB** due to inter-region backbone usage

   ○ **Variable pricing** based on the paired regions

Example: Peering between VNets in East US and West Europe incurs higher costs than East US to East US.

You can view updated pricing on the official AzureVNet pricing page[2].

Cost Estimation with Azure Pricing Calculator

Before implementing peering, use the Azure Pricing Calculator to estimate monthly costs based on projected bandwidth usage.

Steps:

1. Go to theAzure Pricing Calculator[3].
2. Add the **Virtual Network** item.
3. Select **Peering Type** (Regional or Global).
4. Input estimated **monthly GB transfer** per direction.
5. Review the estimated cost.

Alternatively, for scripting and automation, use:

az consumption usage list—start-date 2025-04-01—end-date 2025-04-30—query "[?contains(meterDetails.meterName, 'VNet Peering')]"—output table

This command filters consumption to only show VNet peering-related costs.

Performance Considerations

Latency

One of the biggest performance advantages of VNet peering is **low latency**. Traffic remains within the Azure backbone, avoiding internet hops and unpredictable routing.

---

2. https://azure.microsoft.com/en-us/pricing/details/virtual-network/

3. https://azure.microsoft.com/en-us/pricing/calculator/

- **Regional Peering:** Typically <1 ms latency due to datacenter proximity.

- **Global Peering:** Varies based on physical distance and backbone performance, often 10–100 ms depending on regions.

Use the ping or Test-NetConnection commands from VMs in peered VNets to measure latency:

Test-NetConnection -ComputerName 10.10.2.4 -Port 443

Throughput

Throughput is only limited by:

- **NIC limits** on Azure VMs

- **VM series** (e.g., D-series, F-series)

- **Azure bandwidth quota**

Peering links themselves are **not bottlenecks**, meaning full VM bandwidth can be leveraged.

Monitoring Peering Traffic

Azure provides multiple tools to monitor and optimize traffic over peering connections:

Azure Monitor and Network Watcher

Set up metrics and logs to analyze:

- Peering link usage

- Latency trends
- NSG rule hits and blocked traffic
- Route effectiveness

az network watcher flow-log configure \

—resource-group MyResourceGroup \

—nsg MyNSG \

—enabled true \

—storage-account MyStorageAccount \

—retention 30

Use these logs to calculate usage patterns and identify anomalies or inefficient traffic paths.

Cost Analysis by Resource

Use **Azure Cost Analysis** to break down peering costs by:

- Subscription
- Resource group
- VNet or peering link

This granularity allows budget allocation across departments or environments (e.g., dev vs. prod).

Best Practices for Cost Optimization

1. **Consolidate Services into Shared VNets**

○ Avoid redundant services in multiple VNets by centralizing shared resources in a hub VNet.

○ Reduce inter-VNet communication needs and lower egress costs.

2. **Use Regional Peering Whenever Possible**

○ Design VNets within the same region to reduce cost.

○ Avoid global peering unless absolutely necessary for latency or compliance.

3. **Minimize Cross-Region Chatty Applications**

○ Chatty applications (e.g., databases with high-frequency updates) should be co-located in the same region or VNet.

4. **Use Route Tables to Optimize Traffic Flow**

○ Ensure routes direct traffic over the most efficient (and cost-effective) path.

5. **Enable Compression on Data Transfers**

○ If using custom services to transfer large volumes of data, consider compression to reduce payload size.

6. **Implement Bandwidth Quotas in Applications**

○ Throttle unnecessary data exchange across regions during off-peak hours.

7. **Review and Adjust Regularly**

○ Periodically review peering usage with:

az network watcher connection-monitor list—resource-group MyResourceGroup

This ensures your architecture adapts to changing usage patterns.

Architecture Trade-offs: Performance vs. Cost

Example 1: Regional Microservices Application

- **VNets**: App VNet, DB VNet, Monitoring VNet — all in West Europe
- **Peering**: Regional
- **Latency**: <1 ms
- **Egress cost (per month)**: Minimal

Optimal for high-frequency, performance-sensitive applications.

Example 2: Global SaaS Deployment

- **VNets**: US East (frontend), UK South (backend), Central India (logging)
- **Peering**: Global between all VNets
- **Latency**: 50–100 ms between distant regions

- **Egress cost**: High, depending on GB transferred

Use only if local regulation or failover requirements demand it.

Using Azure Policy to Control Peering Cost Growth

You can enforce organizational standards to reduce peering costs using Azure Policy. For example, block global peering unless explicitly allowed:

```
{
"if": {
"allOf": [
{
"field": "Microsoft.Network/virtualNetworks/virtualNetworkPeerings/remoteVirtualNetwork.location",
"notEquals": "[field('location')]"
}
]
},
"then": {
"effect": "deny"
}
}
```

Apply this policy at the subscription or management group level to prevent unwanted global peering.

Automation for Peering Optimization

Automate cost tracking and alerting with Azure CLI or Logic Apps. Example script to alert on high peering cost:

```
az monitor metrics alert create \

—name PeeringCostAlert \

—resource-group MyResourceGroup \

—scopes /subscriptions/<sub-id>/resourceGroups/MyResourceGroup/providers/Microsoft.Network/virtualNetworks/MyVNet/virtualNetworkPeerings \

—condition "total TransmittedBytes > 10000000000" \

—description "Alert when peering egress exceeds 10 GB"
```

This alerts administrators before significant billing increases occur.

Conclusion

Cost and performance are two sides of the same coin when it comes to Azure VNet peering. While regional peering provides excellent performance at minimal cost, global peering offers broader reach at a premium.

To manage cost effectively:

- Choose regional peering by default.
- Architect with traffic patterns in mind.

- Monitor and optimize regularly.

To ensure performance:

- Monitor latency, throughput, and packet loss.
- Align resource placement with user base and workload profile.

In summary, intelligent planning and ongoing analysis are key to mastering cost and performance in inter-VNet communication. Whether your Azure footprint is local or global, these considerations will help ensure that your network remains both responsive and financially sustainable.

Chapter 4: Hybrid Connectivity Strategies

Connecting On-Premises to Azure: An Overview

As enterprises increasingly adopt the cloud, the need to connect existing on-premises infrastructure with Azure becomes vital. Hybrid connectivity allows businesses to maintain legacy systems while leveraging Azure services, ensuring a seamless, secure, and performant integration between cloud and local resources. This is especially critical for organizations with compliance needs, gradual migration strategies, or systems that cannot be fully moved to the cloud.

This section explores the concepts, methods, and architectures involved in connecting on-premises networks to Azure. It covers connectivity options, security considerations, routing mechanisms, and best practices to ensure resilient and scalable hybrid cloud environments.

What is Hybrid Connectivity?

Hybrid connectivity is the architectural bridge between your **on-premises data center or branch office network** and your **Azure virtual network (VNet)**. It enables:

- **Secure communication** between cloud and local resources
- **Data replication**, backup, and recovery scenarios
- **Hybrid identity** with Azure Active Directory (AD)

- **Multi-tier applications** that span on-premises and Azure environments

Hybrid connectivity is a key enabler for scenarios like lift-and-shift migrations, cloud bursting, remote user access, and centralized policy enforcement.

Key Components of Hybrid Connectivity

To connect your on-premises network to Azure, you'll typically interact with:

- **Azure Virtual Network (VNet)** – The core construct that hosts your cloud infrastructure.
- **VPN Gateway** – Facilitates encrypted tunnels over the public internet.
- **ExpressRoute** – Offers private, dedicated connectivity to Azure.
- **Azure Firewall / NSGs / UDRs** – Security and routing mechanisms that govern hybrid traffic.
- **DNS and DHCP** – Essential for name resolution and IP management across environments.

Each of these elements plays a critical role in ensuring your hybrid setup is secure, performant, and manageable.

Connectivity Options at a Glance

Method	Transport Medium	Latency	Cost	Use Case
Site-to-Site VPN	Public Internet	Medium	Low	Quick setup, branch connectivity
Point-to-Site VPN	Public Internet	Medium	Low	Remote user access
ExpressRoute	Private MPLS	Low	High	Enterprise-grade connectivity

Site-to-Site VPN (S2S VPN)

This is the most common and cost-effective hybrid connectivity method. It connects your on-premises VPN device to an Azure VPN Gateway over an IPsec/IKE tunnel.

Key Features

- Supports both static and dynamic routing (BGP).
- AES 256-bit encryption for data in transit.
- High availability via active-active gateway configuration.
- Up to 1 Gbps bandwidth depending on the SKU.

Sample Setup Using Azure CLI

```
# Create the virtual network gateway

az network vnet-gateway create \
```

—name MyVpnGateway \

—resource-group MyResourceGroup \

—vnet MyVNet \

—public-ip-address MyVpnPublicIP \

—gateway-type Vpn \

—vpn-type RouteBased \

—sku VpnGw1 \

—no-wait

VPN Device Compatibility

Azure supports most industry-standard VPN appliances from Cisco, Juniper, Fortinet, pfSense, and others. Configuration scripts for specific vendors can be downloaded from the Azure portal.

ExpressRoute

Azure ExpressRoute is a premium hybrid connectivity solution that offers private, dedicated connections between your on-premises network and Azure. It bypasses the public internet entirely.

Key Benefits

- **Consistent performance** and low latency.
- **Higher security** since traffic doesn't traverse public networks.
- **Scalability** with bandwidth options up to 100 Gbps.

- **Integration** with Microsoft services like Azure, Office 365, and Dynamics 365.

Use Cases

- Finance, healthcare, and government workloads.
- Applications sensitive to latency and jitter.
- Large-scale data migration and disaster recovery.

Components

- **ExpressRoute Circuit**: Logical connection representing your private link.
- **Peering**:
  - **Private Peering**: Connects directly to Azure VNets.
  - **Microsoft Peering**: Connects to Microsoft services like Office 365.
  - **Public Peering** (Deprecated): Was used for public Azure services access.

Setting Up ExpressRoute

Setting up ExpressRoute requires:

1. Coordination with a service provider.
2. Creating the ExpressRoute circuit.
3. Setting up a connection with Azure Virtual Network via Gateway.

az network express-route create \

—name MyExpressRouteCircuit \

—resource-group MyResourceGroup \

—bandwidth 200 \

—provider Equinix \

—peering-location "Silicon Valley" \

—sku-tier Standard \

—sku-family MeteredData

Then, link to a virtual network using an ExpressRoute gateway.

Routing Between On-Prem and Azure

Routing determines how traffic flows between Azure and on-premises networks. You can use:

- **Static Routing**: Manual definition of routes on both ends.
- **Dynamic Routing with BGP**: Allows Azure and your on-prem router to exchange routes automatically.

User-Defined Routes (UDRs)

You can influence traffic flow in Azure by assigning custom routes to subnets.

az network route-table route create \

—resource-group MyResourceGroup \

—route-table-name MyRouteTable \

—name OnPremRoute \

—address-prefix 10.0.0.0/8 \

—next-hop-type VirtualNetworkGateway

This forces traffic to the 10.0.0.0/8 range to route through the VPN or ExpressRoute.

Security in Hybrid Connectivity

Hybrid connections require careful security planning. Consider the following:

1. **Use Azure Firewall or NVA** for inspecting and filtering inbound and outbound traffic.
2. **Deploy NSGs** to control traffic between subnets and to/from on-prem.
3. **Enable VPN or ExpressRoute encryption** using IPsec/IKE protocols.
4. **Implement Conditional Access and MFA** for identity-based traffic control.
5. **Use Azure Bastion** to connect securely to VMs without exposing RDP/SSH ports.

High Availability and Resiliency

Hybrid architectures must be built with fault tolerance in mind:

- **VPN Gateway Active-Active**: Enable two tunnels for S2S VPN.

- **ExpressRoute Failover**: Use dual circuits across providers or peering locations.
- **Geo-redundant Gateways**: Deploy across regions for disaster recovery.
- **Custom Probes and Load Balancers**: Monitor connectivity health.

Monitoring Hybrid Connectivity

Use Azure Network Watcher to monitor your hybrid links:

- **Connection Monitor**: Track real-time connectivity status.
- **Topology**: Visualizes how on-prem devices connect to Azure.
- **Packet Capture**: Troubleshoot latency or packet loss.
- **Flow Logs**: Capture NSG flows for audit and diagnostics.

Example command:

```
az network watcher connection-monitor create \
—name HybridMonitor \
—resource-group MyResourceGroup \
—location eastus \
```

—source-resource /subscriptions/<sub-id>/resourceGroups/MyResourceGroup/providers/Microsoft.Network/networkInterfaces/nic-1 \

—dest-address 10.1.0.4 \

—protocol Tcp \

—port 443

Best Practices

- **Avoid IP Overlap**: Ensure on-prem and Azure VNets have unique CIDR blocks.
- **Test BGP Configurations**: Validate route propagation with az network vnet-gateway list-learned-routes.
- **Use Shared Gateways** in hub VNets to reduce cost and complexity.
- **Isolate Traffic** using different VNets or subnets for production vs. dev/test.
- **Document Network Diagrams** and keep routing tables updated.

Summary

Connecting your on-premises network to Azure is a foundational step in hybrid cloud adoption. Whether you choose a VPN-based approach for flexibility or ExpressRoute for enterprise performance, your strategy must align with business goals, application requirements, and compliance mandates.

Hybrid connectivity is not just about linking two networks—it's about building a resilient, secure, and agile platform that allows your business to innovate in the cloud while maintaining operational continuity on-premises. By leveraging Azure's tools and services effectively, you can create a seamless bridge between the old and the new, setting the stage for digital transformation at scale.

Site-to-Site VPNs: Configuration and Use Cases

Site-to-Site (S2S) VPN connections are one of the most widely used methods to extend on-premises networks to Azure. They offer a practical, cost-effective, and secure way to bridge the gap between your on-premises data center and cloud-based infrastructure over the public internet using an IPsec/IKE (Internet Protocol Security/ Internet Key Exchange) tunnel.

This section explores the full scope of Site-to-Site VPNs, including their architecture, configuration steps, protocol options, performance tuning, use cases, and troubleshooting techniques. You'll also learn how to integrate S2S VPNs into larger hybrid and enterprise architectures.

What is a Site-to-Site VPN?

A Site-to-Site VPN connects two network infrastructures—typically your on-premises environment and your Azure virtual network—using encrypted tunnels over the public internet. Traffic between the networks remains secure, authenticated, and private.

This method is especially beneficial for:

- Organizations not ready to invest in ExpressRoute.

- Hybrid applications that span cloud and on-premises.
- Short-term projects requiring temporary secure connectivity.
- Branch office access to central services hosted in Azure.

Key Features

- **Encrypted IPsec/IKE tunnel.**
- **Supports static and dynamic routing (via BGP).**
- **Active-passive or active-active configurations.**
- **Bandwidth up to 1.25 Gbps depending on SKU.**
- **Integrates with Network Security Groups and Azure Firewall.**

Architecture Overview

A typical S2S VPN setup involves:

- An **on-premises VPN device or edge router** configured for IPsec/IKE connectivity.
- An **Azure VPN Gateway** deployed in a virtual network with a public IP.
- A **Local Network Gateway** in Azure representing your on-premises IP address space and VPN device.
- **Routing** (static or BGP-based) to enable address reachability.

[On-Prem Firewall/VPN Device] <—IPsec—> [Azure VPN Gateway] <—-> [Azure VNet Resources]

Supported VPN Devices

Azure supports a wide array of third-party VPN devices including:

- Cisco ASA, ISR, and Meraki
- Juniper SRX
- Fortinet FortiGate
- SonicWall
- pfSense
- Ubiquiti EdgeRouter

Azure also provides vendor-specific configuration scripts for many devices through the Azure portal.

Configuration Steps for a Basic Site-to-Site VPN

Below is a comprehensive walkthrough for setting up a S2S VPN connection using the Azure CLI.

Step 1: Create a Virtual Network and Subnet

```
az network vnet create \
—resource-group MyResourceGroup \
—name MyVNet \
—address-prefix 10.1.0.0/16 \
```

—subnet-name GatewaySubnet \

—subnet-prefix 10.1.255.0/27

> Note: The gateway subnet must be named **GatewaySubnet**.

Step 2: Create a Public IP for the VPN Gateway

az network public-ip create \

—resource-group MyResourceGroup \

—name MyVpnPublicIP \

—allocation-method Dynamic

Step 3: Create the VPN Gateway

az network vnet-gateway create \

—resource-group MyResourceGroup \

—name MyVpnGateway \

—public-ip-address MyVpnPublicIP \

—vnet MyVNet \

—gateway-type Vpn \

—vpn-type RouteBased \

—sku VpnGw1 \

—no-wait

Step 4: Define the Local Network Gateway

This step represents your on-premises network.

```
az network local-gateway create \
—resource-group MyResourceGroup \
—name MyLocalGateway \
—gateway-ip-address <ON_PREM_PUBLIC_IP> \
—local-address-prefixes 192.168.0.0/16
```

Step 5: Establish the VPN Connection

```
az network vpn-connection create \
—resource-group MyResourceGroup \
—name MyConnection \
—vnet-gateway1 MyVpnGateway \
—local-gateway2 MyLocalGateway \
—shared-key "MySecretSharedKey"
```

> Ensure the shared key is the same on both ends of the tunnel.

On-Premises Device Configuration

Configure your on-prem device with:

- Azure VPN Gateway IP address

- IKEv2 / IPsec policies
- Shared secret key
- Destination networks (Azure VNet IP range)

Consult your device documentation or use Azure's downloadable scripts for tailored guidance.

Advanced Configuration Options

Active-Active Gateways

For high availability, deploy your VPN Gateway in an **active-active** configuration:

- Requires two public IPs.
- Both tunnels can simultaneously carry traffic.
- Requires BGP to function.

```
az network vnet gateway update \
—resource-group MyResourceGroup \
—name MyVpnGateway \
—enable-active-active true \
—public-ip-addresses MyPublicIP1 MyPublicIP2
```

BGP Support

Border Gateway Protocol (BGP) allows dynamic route exchange between Azure and on-premises devices. It's especially useful in complex networks.

```
az network local-gateway create \

—resource-group MyResourceGroup \

—name MyLocalGateway \

—gateway-ip-address <ON_PREM_IP> \

—local-address-prefixes 0.0.0.0/0 \

—asn 65010 \

—bgp-peering-address 192.168.200.1 \

—peer-weight 0
```

Ensure your VPN Gateway SKU supports BGP (VpnGw1 or higher).

Common Use Cases

Hybrid Cloud Deployments

Organizations often need to maintain legacy on-prem workloads while leveraging Azure for scalability and innovation. S2S VPNs allow seamless communication between both environments, enabling services like Azure AD Connect, file replication, and centralized monitoring.

Branch Office Connectivity

Each branch office can establish its own S2S VPN to a central Azure hub network. This approach reduces latency and centralizes shared services like DNS, identity, and file storage.

Disaster Recovery

S2S VPN can facilitate data synchronization between on-prem and Azure for DR scenarios. Backup solutions like Azure Site Recovery can leverage the VPN to replicate VMs to Azure in near real-time.

Temporary Projects or Migrations

When migrating to Azure, S2S VPNs enable gradual workload movement, allowing resources in both environments to communicate without disruption.

Monitoring and Troubleshooting

Use Azure Network Watcher to monitor tunnel health, performance, and metrics:

az network watcher vpn-connection list-traffic \

—resource-group MyResourceGroup \

—name MyConnection

Common Issues

1. **Tunnel Not Establishing**
   - Check shared keys on both ends.

○ Verify IPsec/IKE policies match.

2. **No Traffic Flow**

○ Validate NSGs and route tables.

○ Confirm your VPN device allows traffic to Azure subnets.

3. **Intermittent Drops**

○ Check for idle timeouts.

○ Upgrade your gateway SKU if hitting throughput limits.

Security Considerations

- **Encryption**: Use strong IKEv2 settings and IPsec policies.
- **Identity**: For user-based access, use Point-to-Site VPNs or Azure AD Conditional Access.
- **Logging**: Enable diagnostic logs for VPN Gateway.
- **Segmentation**: Use subnets and NSGs to restrict unnecessary traffic.
- **Firewall**: Add Azure Firewall or NVA for inspecting hybrid traffic.

Cost Considerations

VPN Gateways are charged per hour based on SKU, plus outbound data transfer. There's no charge for inbound traffic. Shared cost variables include:

- Gateway uptime
- Data transferred out of Azure
- Multi-region transfer if applicable

To estimate costs:

```
az consumption usage list \
—start-date 2025-04-01 \
—end-date 2025-04-30 \
—query "[?contains(meterDetails.meterName, 'VPN Gateway')]" \
—output table
```

Best Practices

- Use **GatewaySubnet** size of /27 or larger to accommodate future scaling.
- Choose a **higher SKU (VpnGw2 or above)** for demanding workloads.
- Implement **redundant VPN tunnels** and gateways for critical services.
- Use **tags and naming conventions** to manage multiple VPN connections.

- **Document all route paths** and verify traffic flow with tools like traceroute.

Summary

Site-to-Site VPNs are a robust, flexible solution for hybrid cloud scenarios. With support for a wide range of devices, protocols, and routing options, they enable businesses to extend on-premises infrastructure into Azure securely and efficiently. From simple development lab connections to enterprise-grade architectures with active-active redundancy and BGP dynamic routing, S2S VPNs provide a foundational path for digital transformation.

With proper configuration, monitoring, and security practices in place, organizations can rely on S2S VPNs to deliver consistent, encrypted, and scalable connectivity across their hybrid environments.

Azure ExpressRoute: Enterprise-Grade Connectivity

Azure ExpressRoute is Microsoft's enterprise-grade solution for establishing private, dedicated network connections between your on-premises infrastructure and Azure. Unlike traditional VPNs that traverse the public internet, ExpressRoute provides a direct link through a connectivity provider, ensuring enhanced performance, reliability, security, and compliance. It is the gold standard for businesses that require consistent latency, high availability, and robust throughput in hybrid and multi-cloud architectures.

This section covers the architecture, setup, operational modes, use cases, monitoring, and optimization strategies for implementing ExpressRoute in Azure-based environments.

Key Features and Benefits

1. Private Connectivity

ExpressRoute connections do not travel over the public internet. This makes them inherently more secure and suitable for sensitive data transfers.

2. High Availability and SLAs

ExpressRoute provides a **99.95% availability SLA** when configured correctly with dual circuits. This makes it ideal for mission-critical workloads.

3. High Throughput

Available bandwidth options range from **50 Mbps to 100 Gbps**, depending on the service provider and SKU, making ExpressRoute suitable for large-scale data migration and replication.

4. Global Reach with ExpressRoute Global Reach

Allows interconnection of your on-prem networks via Microsoft's backbone through Azure.

5. Enhanced Routing with BGP

Supports dynamic route advertisement between on-premises and Azure environments using **BGP (Border Gateway Protocol)**.

6. Multiple Peering Options

- **Private Peering**: Connects to VNets for private address space communication.
- **Microsoft Peering**: Access to Microsoft public services (e.g., Office 365, Azure PaaS).
- **Azure Public Peering**: Now deprecated.

Core Components

An ExpressRoute deployment involves the following key elements:

- **ExpressRoute Circuit**: The logical representation of your connection between Azure and the connectivity provider.
- **Service Provider**: A Microsoft-approved partner who provisions the physical link (e.g., Equinix, BT, AT&T).
- **ExpressRoute Gateway**: An Azure Virtual Network Gateway that supports ExpressRoute and facilitates the connection to your VNet.
- **Peerings**: Configuration that defines the routing paths to Azure services.

Architecture Overview

[On-Prem Router] <——> [Service Provider Edge] <——> [Microsoft Edge] <——> [ExpressRoute Gateway] <——> [Azure VNet]

Provisioning ExpressRoute

Provisioning an ExpressRoute connection involves both Microsoft Azure and your chosen service provider. The process typically involves:

1. **Coordinating with the provider** to establish the physical circuit.
2. **Creating the ExpressRoute circuit in Azure.**
3. **Enabling peerings** (private and/or Microsoft).
4. **Creating and associating the ExpressRoute gateway** with your VNet.
5. **Establishing the connection** between the circuit and the gateway.

Step-by-Step Configuration

Step 1: Create the ExpressRoute Circuit

```
az network express-route create \

—name MyExpressRouteCircuit \

—resource-group MyResourceGroup \

—location "East US" \

—bandwidth 200 \

—provider "Equinix" \

—peering-location "Ashburn" \

—sku-tier Premium \

—sku-family MeteredData
```

- bandwidth in Mbps.
- sku-tier: Standard or Premium (Premium supports Global Reach and more VNets).
- sku-family: MeteredData or UnlimitedData.

Step 2: Obtain Service Key

After creating the circuit, retrieve the **Service Key**, which you provide to your provider for provisioning.

az network express-route show \

—name MyExpressRouteCircuit \

—resource-group MyResourceGroup \

—query serviceKey

Step 3: Set Up Peerings

Private Peering

az network express-route peering create \

—circuit-name MyExpressRouteCircuit \

—peering-type AzurePrivatePeering \

—peer-asn 65010 \

—primary-peer-subnet 192.168.1.0/30 \

—secondary-peer-subnet 192.168.2.0/30 \

—vlan-id 100 \

—resource-group MyResourceGroup

Microsoft Peering (Optional)

Used for services like Azure Blob Storage, Azure SQL, and Office 365.

az network express-route peering create \

—circuit-name MyExpressRouteCircuit \

—peering-type MicrosoftPeering \

—peer-asn 65020 \

—primary-peer-subnet 192.168.3.0/30 \

—secondary-peer-subnet 192.168.4.0/30 \

—vlan-id 200 \

—advertised-public-prefixes 203.0.113.0/24 \

—customer-asn 65020 \

—routing-registry-name ARIN \

—resource-group MyResourceGroup

Step 4: Create ExpressRoute Gateway

az network public-ip create \

—resource-group MyResourceGroup \

—name MyErGatewayPublicIP \

—allocation-method Dynamic

az network vnet-gateway create \

—name MyErGateway \

—public-ip-address MyErGatewayPublicIP \

—resource-group MyResourceGroup \

—vnet MyVNet \

—gateway-type ExpressRoute \

—sku ErGw1AZ \

—no-wait

Step 5: Link the Circuit to the Gateway

az network express-route gateway connection create \

—name MyErConnection \

—resource-group MyResourceGroup \

—express-route-circuit /subscriptions/<sub-id>/resourceGroups/MyResourceGroup/providers/Microsoft.Network/expressRouteCircuits/MyExpressRouteCircuit \

—gateway-name MyErGateway

Use Cases for ExpressRoute

1. Large-Scale Data Migration

High bandwidth and low latency make ExpressRoute ideal for initial cloud migrations involving terabytes or petabytes of data.

2. Enterprise Connectivity for Regulated Industries

Sectors like finance, healthcare, and government require private, auditable connectivity solutions. ExpressRoute enables compliance with standards like ISO 27001, HIPAA, and PCI DSS.

3. Hybrid Architectures with Guaranteed SLAs

Run latency-sensitive applications like SQL Server or SAP HANA in hybrid mode with predictable performance.

4. Global Enterprise Networks

Use **ExpressRoute Global Reach** to interconnect multiple on-prem locations using Azure's network as a WAN backbone.

```
# Example: Link two ExpressRoute circuits

az network express-route peering connection create \

—resource-group MyResourceGroup \

—circuit-name ER-Circuit-EastUS \

—peering-name AzurePrivatePeering \

—peer-circuit-name ER-Circuit-WestEurope \
```

—peer-peering-name AzurePrivatePeering \

—connection-name GlobalLink1

Monitoring and Diagnostics

ExpressRoute Metrics

- Available in Azure Monitor and Log Analytics
- Key metrics:
  - **BytesIn/BytesOut**
  - **BGP Routes Advertised/Received**
  - **Circuit Status**
  - **Availability (SLAs)**

az monitor metrics list \

—resource /subscriptions/<sub-id>/resourceGroups/MyResourceGroup/providers/Microsoft.Network/expressRouteCircuits/MyExpressRouteCircuit \

—metric "BitsInPerSecond"

Network Watcher Support

- Enables **connection monitoring, packet capture**, and **IP flow verification.**
- Useful for validating connectivity and troubleshooting latency or dropouts.

Security Best Practices

- **BGP Filtering**: Prevent route leaks by filtering unnecessary or unverified prefixes.
- **Route Limits**: Implement route limits to prevent prefix flooding.
- **Network Segmentation**: Combine with Azure Firewall and NSGs to limit lateral movement.
- **Authentication and Access Control**: Ensure role-based access and Azure Policy guardrails for ExpressRoute configuration.

Cost Considerations

ExpressRoute pricing is influenced by:

- Circuit bandwidth
- Provider region
- SKU tier (Standard vs. Premium)
- Metered vs. Unlimited data plan
- Number of connected VNets (Premium supports more)

To calculate estimated monthly cost:

```
az costmanagement query usage \

—scope /subscriptions/<sub-id> \
```

—query "[?contains(meterDetails.meterName, 'ExpressRoute')]" \

—output table

Limitations and Design Considerations

- ExpressRoute is **not transitive**—you must design explicitly for multi-VNet or hybrid topologies.
- Some VNets require **gateway transit** via hub VNets to connect through ExpressRoute.
- **Cross-region VNet linking** requires Premium tier.

Summary

Azure ExpressRoute is the premier option for businesses needing private, reliable, and scalable network connectivity between on-premises environments and Azure. With the ability to support large bandwidth, global reach, and strict compliance needs, ExpressRoute plays a critical role in enterprise hybrid strategies.

When properly architected, monitored, and secured, ExpressRoute offers a resilient backbone for modern cloud-first organizations, allowing them to confidently extend their core IT infrastructure into Azure while maintaining enterprise-grade performance and governance.

Network Gateways: VPN vs. ExpressRoute Gateways

In Azure hybrid networking, **network gateways** are the critical junction points that manage traffic between Azure VNets and on-premises environments. Azure supports two main types of gateways: **VPN Gateways** and **ExpressRoute Gateways**. Each is designed for specific connectivity scenarios and comes with distinct capabilities, performance profiles, routing behaviors, and cost models.

Understanding the differences between VPN and ExpressRoute gateways is essential for designing hybrid solutions that meet your organization's reliability, performance, and compliance needs. This section provides a comprehensive comparison of both types, explores their configurations, performance tiers, and operational mechanics, and offers guidance on when and how to use each effectively.

What is a Network Gateway in Azure?

A **network gateway** in Azure is a virtual appliance used to send encrypted traffic between an Azure Virtual Network and another network. This other network may be an on-premises datacenter, a branch office, or another VNet. Gateways are deployed within a dedicated **GatewaySubnet** and support multiple configurations depending on the use case.

Azure provides two gateway types:

- **VPN Gateway** – for secure communication over the internet using IPsec/IKE protocols.
- **ExpressRoute Gateway** – for private connections using Azure ExpressRoute circuits provisioned through a service provider.

Both types share architectural similarities but are optimized for different transport mediums and performance levels.

Comparing VPN Gateway and ExpressRoute Gateway

Feature	VPN Gateway	ExpressRoute Gateway
Transport Medium	Public internet	Private Microsoft Backbone
Tunnel Type	IPsec/IKE (S2S, P2S)	MPLS-based Private Peering
Security	Encrypted over public network	Private by design
Max Bandwidth (approx.)	1.25 Gbps (VpnGw5 SKU)	Up to 10 Gbps (ErGw3AZ SKU)
BGP Support	Yes (from VpnGw1 and above)	Yes
Latency	Variable (internet dependent)	Predictable low-latency
Availability	High (Active-Active possible)	Very High (SLA-backed, dual circuit)
Peering Support	N/A	Private and Microsoft Peering
Setup Time	Quick (hours)	Requires coordination with provider
Cost	Low to moderate	High (based on provider/ circuit)
Ideal Use Cases	SMB, dev/test, branch connectivity	Enterprise-grade workloads, compliance

Gateway SKUs and Performance Tiers

Azure offers a range of SKUs for both VPN and ExpressRoute gateways. Choosing the correct SKU is crucial for performance and cost efficiency.

VPN Gateway SKUs

SKU	Max Throughput	BGP Support	Active-Active	Zone Redundant	Max S2S Tunnels
Basic	~100 Mbps	No	No	No	10
VpnGw1	~650 Mbps	Yes	Yes	No	30
VpnGw2	~1 Gbps	Yes	Yes	Yes	30
VpnGw3	~1.25 Gbps	Yes	Yes	Yes	30
VpnGw5	~1.25 Gbps+	Yes	Yes	Yes	100

ExpressRoute Gateway SKUs

SKU	Max Throughput	VNet Connections	BGP Support	Zone Redundant
ErGw1AZ	~1 Gbps	4	Yes	Yes
ErGw2AZ	~2 Gbps	10	Yes	Yes
ErGw3AZ	~10 Gbps	100	Yes	Yes

Deployment Considerations

Gateway Subnet

For both gateway types, you must define a subnet named **GatewaySubnet** in your VNet:

az network vnet subnet create \

—name GatewaySubnet \

—resource-group MyResourceGroup \

—vnet-name MyVNet \

—address-prefix 10.1.0.0/27

It's recommended to use at least a **/27 subnet** to ensure space for scaling and upgrades.

VPN Gateway Creation

```
az network vnet-gateway create \
—resource-group MyResourceGroup \
—name MyVpnGateway \
—public-ip-address MyVpnPublicIP \
—vnet MyVNet \
—gateway-type Vpn \
—vpn-type RouteBased \
—sku VpnGw2 \
—no-wait
```

ExpressRoute Gateway Creation

```
az network vnet-gateway create \
—resource-group MyResourceGroup \
—name MyErGateway \
—public-ip-address MyErPublicIP \
—vnet MyVNet \
—gateway-type ExpressRoute \
```

—sku ErGw2AZ \

—no-wait

Both gateways can exist in the same VNet if configured properly, allowing you to implement failover strategies.

Use Cases and Decision Matrix

Use VPN Gateway When:

- You need a **quick setup** with minimal cost.
- You want to connect **branch offices** or remote teams.
- Your application can tolerate **variable latency**.
- You're supporting **non-critical** or **development** environments.
- Your provider does not support ExpressRoute or you are in a remote geography.

Use ExpressRoute Gateway When:

- You require **guaranteed throughput and low latency**.
- You handle **sensitive data or compliance-bound workloads.**
- You need to connect to multiple **VNets or on-prem locations.**
- You need access to **Microsoft services** over private peering.

- You're integrating into **global enterprise WANs.**

Routing Considerations

VPN Gateway Routing

- Supports **static routes** and **dynamic routing (BGP)**.
- Use **User Defined Routes (UDRs)** to override default routing when needed.
- Ideal for hub-and-spoke topologies when using multiple site connections.

ExpressRoute Gateway Routing

- Uses **BGP exclusively** for route exchange.
- Requires **route filters** and **prefix advertisements** in Microsoft Peering.
- Can coexist with VPN gateways for redundancy (ExpressRoute + VPN failover).

Redundancy and High Availability

VPN Gateway

- **Active-Active**: Two tunnels operate simultaneously to different on-prem devices.
- **Zone-Redundant**: High availability across availability zones.

ExpressRoute Gateway

- **Dual Circuit Requirement**: SLA applies only when using dual ExpressRoute circuits in different peering locations.

- **Gateway Redundancy**: Use AZ SKUs (e.g., ErGw1AZ) for zone resilience.

Monitoring and Diagnostics

Azure provides multiple tools for tracking gateway performance:

- **Azure Monitor Metrics**:

  - Tunnel status

  - Bytes sent/received

  - BGP session status

- **Azure Network Watcher**:

  - Connection monitor

  - Packet capture

  - IP flow verify

  - VPN diagnostic logs

Example: Monitor gateway bytes in and out

az monitor metrics list \

—resource /subscriptions/<sub-id>/resourceGroups/MyResourceGroup/providers/Microsoft.Network/virtualNetworkGateways/MyVpnGateway \

—metric "TunnelIngressBytes" "TunnelEgressBytes"

Security Best Practices

- Always use **strong shared keys** or **certificates** for VPN authentication.
- Implement **NSGs** and **Azure Firewall** to inspect hybrid traffic.
- Avoid route leaks by **filtering BGP advertisements**.
- Enforce **RBAC roles** and Azure Policy to manage gateway provisioning.

Cost Analysis

VPN Gateway Costs

- Based on the SKU selected (e.g., VpnGw1, VpnGw2).
- Charges for outbound data transfer.
- Inbound data is free.

ExpressRoute Gateway Costs

- Based on SKU and number of VNet connections.

- Additional cost for ExpressRoute circuits (billed separately via provider).

- Premium SKU incurs higher charges for advanced capabilities.

Use the following to track real usage:

az consumption usage list \

—start-date 2025-04-01 \

—end-date 2025-04-30 \

—query "[?contains(meterDetails.meterName, 'Gateway')]" \

—output table

Integration in Enterprise Architectures

In larger hybrid cloud models, both gateway types may be used together. A typical design pattern is:

1. **Primary Connection**: ExpressRoute (high-performance, compliance).
2. **Backup/Failover Connection**: VPN Gateway (low-cost, resilient).

This ensures business continuity even if one path fails, and provides flexibility during migration or provider maintenance events.

Summary

Network gateways are the backbone of Azure's hybrid connectivity architecture. Choosing between a **VPN Gateway** and an

ExpressRoute Gateway depends on your organization's size, performance needs, security requirements, and budget.

While VPN Gateways are easy to set up and ideal for smaller or temporary environments, ExpressRoute Gateways provide the robustness and performance required for enterprise workloads. In some scenarios, using both can yield the best of both worlds—secure, performant, and highly available connectivity for your hybrid cloud landscape.

By carefully selecting the right gateway, configuring it securely, and monitoring its performance, you can ensure a seamless bridge between your on-premises and Azure resources—empowering your business to scale with confidence.

Chapter 5: Securing Your Azure Networks

Azure Firewall: Features and Deployment

Securing network boundaries is a critical aspect of any cloud infrastructure strategy. In Azure, the **Azure Firewall** service offers a fully stateful, scalable, and high-availability solution for controlling and monitoring network traffic. As a cloud-native network security service, it enables you to define and enforce robust traffic filtering rules across your virtual networks with ease. In this section, we'll explore Azure Firewall in-depth—its core features, deployment strategies, integration scenarios, and management practices.

Overview of Azure Firewall

Azure Firewall is a **PaaS (Platform-as-a-Service)** solution that acts as a centralized firewall across your Azure environment. It provides layer 3 to layer 7 traffic filtering, fully integrated with the Azure Monitor for logging and analytics.

Key Features:

- **Stateful packet inspection** for both inbound and outbound traffic
- **High availability** without requiring load balancer configuration
- **Built-in auto-scaling** to handle varying traffic loads
- **Threat intelligence-based filtering** from Microsoft Threat Intelligence feed

- **Application rules** and **network rules** to control traffic
- **Integration with Azure Policy** and **Azure Monitor**

Deployment Scenarios

There are multiple ways Azure Firewall can be deployed depending on your architectural needs. The most common approaches include:

Hub-and-Spoke Architecture

Azure Firewall is typically deployed in a **centralized Hub VNet**, while other application and resource networks are deployed in **Spoke VNets**. Traffic from the spokes is routed to the firewall in the hub via **User-Defined Routes (UDRs)**.

Benefits:

- Centralized policy management
- Simplified logging and analytics
- Easy to enforce compliance standards

Single VNet Architecture

In smaller environments or isolated environments, Azure Firewall can be deployed in a **single VNet**, protecting the resources within that VNet only. This is useful for isolated workloads with strict security requirements.

Provisioning Azure Firewall via the Azure Portal

1. Navigate to **Azure Portal** > **Create a Resource** > Search for **Azure Firewall**

2. Select **Create**

3. Fill in basic configuration:

○ **Name**

○ **Region**

○ **Resource Group**

○ **Virtual Network** (Hub VNet ideally)

4. Choose or create a **Public IP Address**

5. Select **Availability Zones** if required

6. Click **Review + Create** and deploy

Once deployed, you'll configure **Rules** and **Routing** to make the firewall effective.

Azure Firewall Rule Types

Azure Firewall uses two primary types of rules to filter traffic:

Network Rules

These rules operate at **Layer 3 & 4** and are useful for non-HTTP/S traffic (e.g., RDP, FTP, SSH).

Example:

Name: Allow-RDP

Protocol: TCP

Source Address: 10.0.0.0/24

Destination Address: 192.168.0.4

Destination Port: 3389

Action: Allow

Application Rules

These are **Layer 7** rules and work with fully qualified domain names (FQDNs), ideal for controlling HTTP/HTTPS traffic.

Example:

Name: Allow-GitHub

Source: 10.0.0.0/24

Target FQDN: *.github.com

Protocol: HTTPS

Action: Allow

You can group multiple rules into **Rule Collections**, and assign a priority to them. Collections are evaluated based on priority and stop processing once a match is found.

Route Configuration and Integration

After creating firewall rules, the next step is **traffic routing**. You'll use **User-Defined Routes (UDRs)** to ensure traffic is forced through the Azure Firewall.

1. Go to the **Route Table** in the Azure Portal

2. Create a new route:

   - **Name:** To-Firewall
   - **Address Prefix:** 0.0.0.0/0
   - **Next Hop Type:** Virtual Appliance
   - **Next Hop Address:** Private IP of Azure Firewall

3. Associate the route table with the subnet hosting the workload

This setup ensures all outbound (and optionally inbound) traffic passes through the firewall for inspection and logging.

Azure Firewall Premium

For more advanced use cases, **Azure Firewall Premium** adds capabilities such as:

- **TLS inspection**
- **Intrusion detection and prevention system (IDPS)**
- **Web categories for URL filtering**
- **Advanced threat intelligence**

These features enable **deep packet inspection**, allowing greater control over encrypted and application-layer traffic. Premium SKUs are especially useful in regulated industries such as **finance**, **healthcare**, and **government**.

Logging and Monitoring

Azure Firewall integrates natively with **Azure Monitor**, **Log Analytics**, and **Event Hubs** for centralized logging and analytics.

To enable diagnostics:

1. Go to the Azure Firewall resource
2. Select **Diagnostics Settings**
3. Enable and select:
    - **AzureFirewallApplicationRule**
    - **AzureFirewallNetworkRule**
    - **AzureFirewallDnsProxy**
    - **AzureFirewallThreatIntel**

Logs can be queried in **Log Analytics** using Kusto Query Language (KQL):

```
AzureDiagnostics

| where Category == "AzureFirewallNetworkRule"

| project TimeGenerated, msg_s, src_ip_s, dest_ip_s, action_s
```

These insights can be used for:

- Alerting
- Forensics
- Policy refinement
- Traffic pattern analysis

Cost Considerations

Azure Firewall pricing consists of:

- **Fixed hourly fee** for deployment
- **Per GB processed** (inbound + outbound)

Premium SKU comes at a higher fixed and variable rate, justified by additional security features.

Tip: To reduce costs:

- Minimize unnecessary traffic via NSGs before it hits the firewall
- Use caching and CDN where applicable
- Offload TLS termination to Application Gateway where possible

---

Azure Firewall vs Network Security Groups (NSGs)

Feature	Azure Firewall	NSG
Layer	L3–L7	L3–L4
Stateful	Yes	Yes
FQDN filtering	Yes (Premium for HTTPS)	No
Threat Intelligence	Yes	No
Centralized Logging	Yes	Limited
Application Filtering	Yes	No

Use **NSGs for local subnet-level filtering**, and **Azure Firewall for centralized, enterprise-grade protection.**

Best Practices for Azure Firewall

- **Deploy in a Hub-and-Spoke topology** for central control
- **Combine with NSGs** for defense in depth
- **Use application rules wherever possible** to minimize attack surface
- **Enable diagnostics and alerts**
- **Review logs regularly and refine rules**
- **Keep your threat intelligence mode on 'Alert and Deny'**
- **Automate deployment using Infrastructure as Code**

Automating Deployment with Bicep

You can deploy Azure Firewall using Bicep templates for repeatability:

```
resource firewall 'Microsoft.Network/azureFirewalls@2022-01-01' = {

name: 'myFirewall'

location: resourceGroup().location

properties: {

sku: {

name: 'AZFW_VNet'

tier: 'Standard'

}

ipConfigurations: [

{

name: 'azureFirewallIpConfig'

properties: {

subnet: {

id: subnetResource.id

}

publicIPAddress: {

id: publicIp.id
```

```
}
}
}
]
}
}
```

Summary

Azure Firewall is a cornerstone of modern, cloud-native security strategies in Azure. Its ability to provide deep, centralized visibility and control across virtual networks makes it invaluable in enterprise environments. By combining it with other Azure services like NSGs, Application Gateway, and Log Analytics, organizations can enforce robust, scalable, and manageable security postures. Deploying Azure Firewall effectively requires thoughtful planning, automation, and regular review—but the outcome is a secure and compliant cloud network.

Application Gateway and Web Application Firewall (WAF)

The Azure Application Gateway is a powerful Layer 7 load balancer that allows you to manage web traffic effectively for your applications. One of its most compelling features is its integration with the **Web Application Firewall (WAF)**, which offers centralized protection against common web vulnerabilities such as SQL injection, cross-site scripting (XSS), and other threats defined by the OWASP Top 10.

In this section, we'll explore the Application Gateway in detail, focusing on its architecture, configuration options, WAF modes, security capabilities, and real-world deployment patterns. We will also cover how it fits into a broader network security strategy, including automation and monitoring.

Azure Application Gateway Overview

Azure Application Gateway operates at **Layer 7 (HTTP/HTTPS)** of the OSI model. Unlike traditional load balancers, which route traffic based on IP and port, the Application Gateway can make routing decisions based on URI path or host headers.

Key Features:

- SSL termination
- Cookie-based session affinity
- URL-based routing
- Multi-site hosting
- Web Application Firewall (WAF)
- Autoscaling and zone redundancy
- Custom probes for health monitoring

Architecture and Components

An Application Gateway is made up of several components:

- **Frontend IP Configuration**: Public or private IP address for client traffic

- **Listeners**: Define protocols and ports
- **Backend Pools**: Targets (VMs, VMSS, App Services)
- **Routing Rules**: Direct traffic based on patterns
- **HTTP Settings**: Configure health probes, timeouts, and backend ports
- **WAF Policy**: Enables and configures the Web Application Firewall

Application Gateway supports both **Standard** and **WAF-enabled** SKUs. WAF-enabled SKUs are required to enforce rules for application-layer security.

Provisioning Application Gateway with WAF

To create an Application Gateway with WAF enabled via the Azure Portal:

1. Navigate to **Create a Resource** > **Application Gateway**
2. Select **WAF (Web Application Firewall)** as the tier
3. Choose the appropriate **WAF mode** (Detection or Prevention)
4. Create or select a **Virtual Network** with at least two subnets:
    - One for the Application Gateway
    - One for the backend pool (e.g., App Services, VMs)

5. Assign a **Frontend IP configuration**

6. Configure **Listeners, Routing Rules, HTTP settings,** and **Backend pools**

7. Apply a **WAF policy** if desired or configure later

8. Review and create

WAF Modes and Configuration

Azure WAF operates in two modes:

- **Detection Mode**: Logs all requests and actions taken by the WAF without blocking
- **Prevention Mode**: Actively blocks requests that match WAF rules

You can configure the WAF to use the **OWASP Core Rule Set (CRS)**. As of now, Azure WAF supports **CRS 3.2** and **CRS 3.1.**

Example of enabling a WAF policy via PowerShell:

```
$wafPolicy = New-AzApplicationGatewayWebApplicationFirewallPolicy -Name "MyWAFPolicy" `

-ResourceGroupName "MyResourceGroup" `

-Location "EastUS" `

-CustomRules @() `

-ManagedRules @(
```

```
@{
RuleSetType = "OWASP";
RuleSetVersion = "3.2";
}
)
```

Custom Rules can be used to tailor WAF behavior, e.g., block a specific IP range:

```
{
"name": "BlockMaliciousIP",
"priority": 100,
"ruleType": "MatchRule",
"action": "Block",
"matchConditions": [
{
"matchVariables": [
{
"variableName": "RemoteAddr"
}
],
"operator": "IPMatch",
"matchValues": [
```

```
"203.0.113.0/24"
]
}
]
}
```

Common Use Cases for Application Gateway with WAF

Multi-site Hosting

Allows multiple domains to be hosted on the same gateway. Each listener routes requests based on the host header.

Path-Based Routing

Use URI-based routing to direct traffic to different backend pools:

- /api → App Service A
- /frontend → App Service B

SSL Termination

The gateway can decrypt incoming SSL requests and forward them unencrypted to the backend, offloading computational overhead.

Application Gateway vs Azure Front Door vs Load Balancer

Feature	Application Gateway	Azure Front Door	Azure Load Balancer
OSI Layer	7	7	4
Web Application Firewall	Yes	Yes	No
SSL Offloading	Yes	Yes	No
URL-based Routing	Yes	Yes	No
Regional/Global	Regional	Global	Regional
Protocol Support	HTTP/ HTTPS	HTTP/ HTTPS	TCP/UDP

Use **Application Gateway** when you need in-region web traffic routing and WAF, **Front Door** for global distribution with acceleration, and **Load Balancer** for L4-based workloads.

Monitoring and Logging

Azure Application Gateway offers deep integration with **Azure Monitor**, **Log Analytics**, and **Network Watcher**.

Enable diagnostics to log:

- WAF logs
- Performance metrics
- Backend health statuses
- Request processing errors

Sample KQL query to analyze WAF blocks:

AzureDiagnostics

| where Category == "ApplicationGatewayFirewallLog"

| where action_s == "Blocked"

| summarize Count = count() by clientIP_s, ruleSetType_s, ruleId_s, Message

These logs can help identify patterns of malicious traffic or misconfigurations in your WAF rules.

Autoscaling and Performance Tuning

Application Gateway supports autoscaling based on:

- Number of connections
- CPU utilization
- Request rate

This ensures high availability during traffic spikes. However, it's important to configure **custom probes** for accurate health checks.

Example Probe Settings:

- Protocol: HTTPS
- Path: /healthcheck
- Timeout: 30 seconds
- Interval: 30 seconds

- Unhealthy Threshold: 3

These settings ensure backend instances are only routed traffic when verified to be healthy.

Automation with ARM Templates

To automate the deployment of Application Gateway with WAF, use an ARM template:

```
{
"type": "Microsoft.Network/applicationGateways",
"apiVersion": "2021-03-01",
"name": "myAppGateway",
"location": "[resourceGroup().location]",
"properties": {
"sku": {
"name": "WAF_v2",
"tier": "WAF_v2",
"capacity": 2
},
"gatewayIPConfigurations": [...],
"frontendIPConfigurations": [...],
"frontendPorts": [...],
"backendAddressPools": [...],
```

```
"backendHttpSettingsCollection": [...],
"httpListeners": [...],
"urlPathMaps": [...],
"requestRoutingRules": [...],
"webApplicationFirewallConfiguration": {
"enabled": true,
"firewallMode": "Prevention",
"ruleSetType": "OWASP",
"ruleSetVersion": "3.2"
}
}
}
```

Best Practices

- **Use Prevention Mode** in production; Detection mode is for testing
- Regularly **update the OWASP CRS version**
- Configure **custom rules** for known malicious actors
- Use **path-based routing** for microservices-based applications
- Enable **HTTPS-only access** for all listeners

- Keep the **WAF policy version consistent** across environments
- Regularly **analyze WAF logs** to fine-tune policies

Real-World Deployment Scenario

A healthcare organization deploying multiple internal services behind an Azure Application Gateway with WAF uses:

- **Multiple listeners** for API and patient portal
- **Path-based routing** for various microservices
- **WAF custom rules** to block known scanners and specific user agents
- **SSL termination** on the gateway
- **Log forwarding** to Sentinel for threat detection

This setup allows the organization to maintain strict compliance (e.g., HIPAA) while supporting scalable and secure web access.

Summary

Azure Application Gateway with integrated WAF is a vital component for any cloud-first organization that relies on secure, reliable web access. Its Layer 7 intelligence, support for custom routing, autoscaling, and web protection makes it ideal for modern application architectures. Whether you're hosting a single web app or a suite of microservices, the Application Gateway enables robust, centralized traffic management and application-layer security.

Through proper planning, monitoring, and automation, it significantly enhances the defense posture of your Azure workloads.

DDoS Protection in Azure

Distributed Denial of Service (DDoS) attacks are a growing threat in today's connected world, capable of disrupting services, exhausting resources, and impacting business continuity. Azure offers robust, native protection against such attacks through **Azure DDoS Protection**, a comprehensive platform security service that safeguards applications by absorbing and mitigating DDoS attack traffic before it can impact application availability.

In this section, we will explore how Azure DDoS Protection works, its two service tiers, integration with other Azure services, how to configure and monitor it, best practices, and real-world scenarios. Whether you're protecting a web application, an API, or mission-critical infrastructure, understanding and implementing Azure DDoS Protection is an essential component of your Azure network security strategy.

Understanding DDoS Attacks

A DDoS attack floods a network or application with traffic from multiple sources, rendering services unavailable to legitimate users. These attacks come in various forms:

- **Volumetric Attacks**: Exhaust bandwidth by flooding with large amounts of traffic.

- **Protocol Attacks**: Exploit weaknesses in layer 3/4 protocols like SYN floods or fragmented packet attacks.

- **Application-Layer Attacks**: Target HTTP/HTTPS and DNS services to exhaust server resources.

Azure DDoS Protection defends against all these categories by detecting and mitigating abnormal traffic patterns in real-time using the scale and capacity of Microsoft's global network.

Azure DDoS Protection Tiers

Azure offers two primary tiers:

Basic (Always-On, Included)

- Automatically enabled on all Azure public IPs
- Provides protection against common network-level attacks
- Integrated with the Azure global infrastructure
- No configuration or monitoring features

Standard (Advanced, Configurable)

- Provides additional detection and mitigation capabilities
- Includes telemetry, alerting, and mitigation flow logs
- Custom policy tuning per virtual network
- SLA-backed protection with cost guarantee

- Integration with Azure Firewall, App Gateway, and third-party services

---

Key Features of DDoS Protection Standard

- **Adaptive tuning**: Learns baseline traffic for each protected IP and dynamically adjusts thresholds.

- **Mitigation policies**: Automatically triggers DDoS mitigation when attack thresholds are breached.

- **Attack analytics**: Detailed logs and metrics via Azure Monitor and Log Analytics.

- **Cost protection**: Service Credit Protection covers scale-out charges during a verified DDoS attack.

- **Rapid response**: Microsoft's DDoS Rapid Response (DRR) team is available during an attack for assistance.

Enabling Azure DDoS Protection Standard

Azure DDoS Protection Standard is enabled at the **Virtual Network (VNet)** level. All public IP addresses attached to resources in that VNet are automatically protected.

Using Azure Portal:

1. Navigate to **Create a resource > Networking > DDoS Protection Plan**
2. Choose a name, region, and resource group
3. Create the plan

4. Navigate to your **Virtual Network**
5. Select **DDoS Protection** under **Settings**
6. Associate the protection plan

Using Azure CLI:

```
# Create a DDoS Protection Plan

az network ddos-protection create \

—resource-group MyResourceGroup \

—name MyDdosPlan

# Associate plan with a VNet

az network vnet update \

—name MyVnet \

—resource-group MyResourceGroup \

—ddos-protection-plan /subscriptions/{sub-id}/resourceGroups/MyResourceGroup/providers/Microsoft.Network/ddosProtectionPlans/MyDdosPlan
```

Monitoring and Diagnostics

Once enabled, you can access telemetry and diagnostics via **Azure Monitor**, **Log Analytics**, and **Network Watcher**.

Recommended metrics:

- UnderDDoSAttack: Indicates whether your resource is currently under attack

- PacketsDroppedDDoS: Number of packets dropped due to DDoS mitigation

- InboundPacketsRate: Incoming packet rate

- SynRate: Rate of SYN packets (useful for identifying SYN flood attacks)

Sample KQL to detect active attacks:

AzureDiagnostics

| where Category == "DDoSProtectionNotifications"

| where OperationName == "DDoSMitigationStarted"

| project TimeGenerated, Resource, OperationName, AttackVector_s, SourceIP_s

Azure also generates alerts that you can configure to trigger actions via email, webhooks, or integration with Azure Sentinel or Logic Apps.

Integration with Other Azure Services

Azure DDoS Protection integrates seamlessly with other security services:

- **Azure Firewall**: Protects application ports from unauthorized access

- **Application Gateway with WAF**: Protects Layer 7 against web attacks

- **Azure Front Door**: Works with global edge to mitigate volumetric and app-layer attacks

- **Private Endpoints**: Reduce public exposure where applicable

- **NSGs**: Enforce port/protocol filtering and segment traffic

A layered defense approach that includes DDoS Protection at the edge, combined with per-service protections internally, significantly increases resilience.

Example: Protecting a Web Application

Imagine a publicly accessible Azure App Service protected behind an Application Gateway and Azure Firewall. The Application Gateway is in a dedicated VNet with an associated DDoS Protection Plan.

1. Public IP on App Gateway → DDoS Standard defends this IP
2. App Gateway → WAF protects against app-layer vulnerabilities
3. Azure Firewall → Filters traffic before reaching backend
4. NSGs → Enforce least-privilege access on backend subnets

This layered setup mitigates DDoS, exploits, malformed packets, and unauthorized access.

Cost and SLA Considerations

Azure DDoS Protection Standard is billed per protected VNet and includes:

- Flat monthly fee per protection plan

- Unlimited protected IPs in the associated VNets

- Cost guarantee for service credit reimbursement during verified attacks

SLA: Microsoft guarantees 99.99% availability for DDoS Protection services and supports cost reimbursements for scale-out of Azure services during attacks.

Best Practices for Azure DDoS Protection

- **Enable DDoS Protection Standard** for all VNets hosting public-facing resources

- **Use custom alerts** based on attack patterns and threshold metrics

- **Integrate logging with SIEM tools** like Azure Sentinel for incident correlation

- **Periodically review traffic baselines** to ensure tuning is effective

- **Leverage DRR team** during suspected or ongoing attacks

- **Use public IP address SKU as "Standard"** for compatibility

- **Simulate attacks in test environments** to validate mitigation and alerting

---

Simulating and Testing DDoS Scenarios

While Azure does not allow customers to launch real DDoS attacks against production services, **test environments** can be used to simulate:

- High-rate SYN floods
- UDP amplification patterns
- Application-level stress testing

Use third-party simulation tools in a controlled, isolated environment, and monitor:

- Alerts raised
- Packets dropped
- Latency impacts
- Scaling events

This validates your readiness without putting live systems at risk.

Incident Response and Mitigation Workflow

In the event of a DDoS attack, Azure's mitigation process typically follows these steps:

1. **Detection**: Anomaly is identified via traffic thresholds
2. **Mitigation Initiated**: Traffic is rerouted through scrubbing centers
3. **Traffic Filtering**: Attack traffic is dropped, clean traffic continues

4. **Notification**: Alerts are pushed to Azure Monitor
5. **Post-Attack Analytics**: Logs and telemetry are available for forensic review

If you're on the DDoS Standard plan, you can also contact the **Microsoft DDoS Rapid Response (DRR)** team for active help.

Summary

Azure DDoS Protection is a vital, scalable, and intelligent defense mechanism that ensures your applications remain resilient and available in the face of modern attack vectors. With its always-on nature, integration with other Azure services, deep telemetry, and cost guarantees, it offers both security and peace of mind for developers, operations teams, and stakeholders. By implementing a layered defense strategy and proactively monitoring traffic, you can confidently secure your services against one of the most disruptive forms of cyber threats.

Zero Trust Networking in Azure

The traditional network security model of "trust but verify" is no longer sufficient in today's world of hybrid work, mobile access, and increasingly sophisticated cyber threats. **Zero Trust** is a modern security framework that assumes breach and explicitly verifies every request, regardless of its origin. In Azure, Zero Trust networking enables organizations to build secure, scalable environments by enforcing strict access controls, continuous verification, and minimizing implicit trust across the infrastructure.

This section provides an in-depth exploration of Zero Trust Networking in Azure. We'll look at the principles behind Zero Trust, how Azure supports them across identity, network, and endpoints, and how to implement a Zero Trust architecture using Azure-native tools and services. We'll also include automation examples and monitoring practices that reinforce Zero Trust principles across the entire stack.

Core Principles of Zero Trust

Zero Trust is not a single product but a **comprehensive security strategy** built on three key principles:

1. **Verify Explicitly** – Always authenticate and authorize based on all available data points (identity, location, device health, service, data classification, etc.)
2. **Use Least Privilege Access** – Limit user and application access to only the permissions they need, just-in-time and just-enough-access.
3. **Assume Breach** – Design security with the assumption that your environment is already compromised.

Azure brings these principles to life through services such as Azure Active Directory, Conditional Access, Azure Firewall, NSGs, Azure Policy, Microsoft Defender for Cloud, and many others.

Identity as the Security Perimeter

In a Zero Trust model, **identity** is the new perimeter. Azure enables strong identity verification and access control using:

- **Azure Active Directory (AAD)** – Centralized identity management and SSO

- **Multi-Factor Authentication (MFA)** – Reduces the risk of credential compromise

- **Conditional Access Policies** – Enforce access based on conditions like device state, user risk, or location
- **Privileged Identity Management (PIM)** – Just-in-time access for administrators

Example: Conditional Access Policy via PowerShell

```
Connect-AzureAD

New-AzureADMSConditionalAccessPolicy -DisplayName "Block legacy auth" `

-State "enabled" `

-Conditions @{

SignInRiskLevels = @("high")

ClientAppTypes = @("Other")

} `

-GrantControls @{

BuiltInControls = @("Block")

}
```

This policy blocks legacy client applications for users identified as high-risk during sign-in.

Securing the Network Plane

Zero Trust Networking in Azure includes network-level segmentation, strict access controls, and eliminating unnecessary exposure.

Key Network Security Tools:

- **Network Security Groups (NSGs)** – Stateless firewall rules at subnet and NIC level
- **Azure Firewall** – Stateful traffic filtering with L3-L7 visibility
- **Azure Application Gateway with WAF** – Protects web applications from OWASP threats
- **Private Endpoints** – Isolate services within your VNet
- **Azure Bastion** – Secure RDP/SSH without public IPs

NSG Example – Deny All Inbound Except Specific Ports

```
{
"name": "deny-all-inbound",
"properties": {
"priority": 4096,
"direction": "Inbound",
"access": "Deny",
"protocol": "*",
"sourcePortRange": "*",
"destinationPortRange": "*",
"sourceAddressPrefix": "*",
"destinationAddressPrefix": "*"
```

}

}

Always combine broad "deny" rules with narrow "allow" rules earlier in the rule set to permit only approved communication.

Micro-Segmentation in Azure

Traditional segmentation divides networks into large trust zones. Zero Trust takes segmentation further through **micro-segmentation**, isolating workloads at a fine-grained level.

Azure supports micro-segmentation via:

- **Subnets and NSGs** per workload type or environment (e.g., web tier, app tier, DB tier)
- **Application Security Groups (ASGs)** – Logical grouping of VMs for simplified rule management
- **User-Defined Routes (UDRs)** – Custom traffic routing for layered inspection

Example: Allow Only Web Servers to Talk to App Servers via ASG

{

"name": "AllowWebToApp",

"properties": {

"priority": 100,

"direction": "Inbound",

```
"access": "Allow",

"protocol": "Tcp",

"sourceApplicationSecurityGroups": [{ "id": "/subscriptions/xxx/resourceGroups/rg/providers/Microsoft.Network/applicationSecurityGroups/web-asg" }],

"destinationApplicationSecurityGroups": [{ "id": "/subscriptions/xxx/resourceGroups/rg/providers/Microsoft.Network/applicationSecurityGroups/app-asg" }],

"sourcePortRange": "*",

"destinationPortRange": "443"

}

}
```

This enforces communication only between designated groups, reducing lateral movement potential.

Device and Endpoint Security

Devices and endpoints form another attack surface. Azure integrates with **Microsoft Defender for Endpoint**, **Intune**, and **Azure AD Conditional Access** to ensure secure device compliance.

Common policies include:

- Requiring compliant devices
- Blocking access from rooted/jailbroken devices
- Enforcing Windows Defender Antivirus and BitLocker

- Requiring up-to-date OS versions

Conditional Access Rule Example: Require Compliant Devices

```
New-AzureADMSConditionalAccessPolicy -DisplayName "Require compliant devices" `
-State "enabled" `
-Conditions @{
Users = @{
IncludeUsers = @("All")
}
} `
-GrantControls @{
BuiltInControls = @("RequireCompliantDevice")
}
```

This blocks access unless the device is enrolled in Intune and meets compliance policies.

Data and Application Layer Security

Zero Trust extends beyond the network to data and applications:

- **Azure Information Protection** – Labels and encrypts sensitive data
- **Microsoft Purview** – Tracks data flows and enforces governance

- **Managed Identities** – Avoids hardcoded credentials in apps
- **Key Vault** – Centralizes key, secret, and certificate management

Use **Azure Policy** to enforce best practices like encryption-at-rest, HTTPS-only access, and private endpoint usage.

Example: Azure Policy to Enforce HTTPS

```
{
"if": {
"allOf": [
{
"field": "type",
"equals": "Microsoft.Web/sites"
},
{
"field": "Microsoft.Web/sites/httpsOnly",
"equals": "false"
}
]
},
"then": {
```

```
"effect": "deny"
}
}
```

This prevents creation of web apps without HTTPS enforcement.

Logging, Monitoring, and Incident Response

A Zero Trust architecture must continuously log and monitor all access. Azure offers a unified view through:

- **Microsoft Defender for Cloud** – Threat protection and recommendations
- **Azure Monitor & Log Analytics** – Collect and query logs across services
- **Azure Sentinel** – SIEM and SOAR for incident detection and automation
- **Activity Logs and Alerts** – Monitor administrative changes and suspicious events

Sample KQL: Find Failed Sign-ins from External IPs

```
SigninLogs
| where ResultType != 0
| where Location !in ("YourCountry")
| project UserPrincipalName, IPAddress, Location, ResultDescription, TimeGenerated
```

Enable **just-in-time VM access** in Defender for Cloud to reduce the attack surface and log any administrative access attempts.

Automating Zero Trust with Infrastructure as Code

Zero Trust can and should be codified using tools such as **ARM templates, Bicep**, and **Terraform.**

Bicep Example: Secure VNet with Firewall and Private DNS

```
resource vnet 'Microsoft.Network/virtualNetworks@2022-01-01' ={

name: 'secureVnet'

location: resourceGroup().location

properties: {

addressSpace: {

addressPrefixes: ['10.0.0.0/16']

}

subnets: [

{

name: 'firewallSubnet'

properties: {

addressPrefix: '10.0.1.0/24'

delegations: []

}
```

```
}
]
}
}
```

Combine with Azure Policy assignments to enforce compliance, and use Azure DevOps pipelines for continuous security deployment.

Real-World Architecture: Zero Trust in Action

A financial services firm implements Zero Trust across its cloud infrastructure:

- All employees authenticate using Azure AD with MFA
- Conditional Access policies enforce compliant, managed devices
- Workloads are segmented into VNets with NSGs and ASGs
- No public IPs; access is routed through Azure Firewall and Application Gateway
- Private Endpoints are used for storage and databases
- Defender for Cloud provides continuous threat protection
- Azure Sentinel monitors anomalies and triggers automated responses

This architecture ensures that even if a credential is compromised or an endpoint is infected, the attacker's movement is constrained and visible.

Summary

Zero Trust is a mindset and a security framework that reshapes how access and trust are granted in modern cloud environments. In Azure, Zero Trust is deeply integrated into identity, networking, data, and operational layers, offering comprehensive defense against both internal and external threats.

By adopting Azure-native tools such as Conditional Access, Azure Firewall, NSGs, Private Endpoints, and Defender for Cloud—and enforcing consistent policies through Infrastructure as Code—you can build a robust, future-proof security architecture. The key to Zero Trust is continuous evaluation, logging, and adaptability, turning your Azure environment into a resilient, verifiable, and trustworthy platform for digital transformation.

Chapter 6: Advanced Connectivity Scenarios

Hub-and-Spoke Topology Design

The **hub-and-spoke topology** is a widely adopted network architecture in Azure that provides a scalable and secure approach to interconnecting various workloads, managing centralized services, and enforcing security boundaries. This model enables organizations to design their networks in a modular fashion, allowing for clear segregation of duties, simplified management, and better cost and policy enforcement.

In Azure, the **hub** acts as the central point of connectivity, while **spokes** are VNets that host individual workloads or environments such as development, staging, or production. Spokes typically do not communicate with each other directly but instead route their traffic through the hub, where centralized services like firewalls, DNS, and VPN gateways reside.

Benefits of Hub-and-Spoke Topology

Implementing a hub-and-spoke architecture in Azure yields multiple advantages:

- **Centralized management**: Core services such as DNS, NTP, and identity can be deployed in the hub and shared.
- **Improved security**: All ingress and egress traffic is inspected and controlled through a central firewall or Application Gateway.

- **Scalability**: New spokes can be added without redesigning the entire network.
- **Cost control**: Avoid redundant deployment of shared services across VNets.
- **Simplified routing**: Traffic flows can be more easily managed and monitored.
- **Isolation**: Spokes are isolated from each other, reducing lateral movement in case of compromise.

Designing the Hub

The **hub VNet** contains the shared services and connectivity mechanisms used across all environments. These typically include:

- **Azure Firewall or NVA (Network Virtual Appliance)**
- **VPN Gateway and/or ExpressRoute Gateway**
- **Azure Bastion**
- **Private DNS Zones**
- **Log Analytics agents**
- **Jumpbox or Bastion Host for administrative access**

A sample CIDR range for a hub could be 10.0.0.0/16, with subnets like:

- 10.0.1.0/24 – GatewaySubnet
- 10.0.2.0/24 – Azure Firewall subnet

- 10.0.3.0/24 – Bastion subnet
- 10.0.4.0/24 – Shared services

Each subnet should be isolated using **NSGs** and optionally **ASGs** to control traffic between resources.

Designing the Spokes

Spoke VNets host the actual applications, VMs, App Services, databases, etc. Each spoke typically represents an environment (e.g., dev, test, prod) or a business unit.

Spokes use **VNet Peering** to connect to the hub. Peering allows low-latency, high-throughput communication between VNets in the same region or globally.

Spoke CIDRs should be non-overlapping and manageable:

- 10.1.0.0/16 – Dev environment
- 10.2.0.0/16 – Staging
- 10.3.0.0/16 – Production

Each spoke contains its own internal segmentation (web/app/db) using subnets and NSGs.

Configuring VNet Peering

Peering must be configured **bidirectionally** between each spoke and the hub.

Azure CLI Example

```
# Peer Hub to Spoke

az network vnet peering create \

—name HubToDevSpoke \

—resource-group NetworkingRG \

—vnet-name HubVNet \

—remote-vnet DevSpokeVNetID \

—allow-vnet-access

# Peer Spoke to Hub

az network vnet peering create \

—name DevSpokeToHub \

—resource-group DevRG \

—vnet-name DevSpokeVNet \

—remote-vnet HubVNetID \

—allow-vnet-access \

—allow-forwarded-traffic
```

Set allow-forwarded-traffic to true if traffic is being routed through a firewall or other device in the hub.

User-Defined Routes (UDRs)

Routing in hub-and-spoke architecture is typically handled via **User-Defined Routes**. Spokes should have route tables that send **all egress traffic** (0.0.0.0/0) and inter-VNet traffic to the Azure Firewall in the hub.

UDR Example

Destination	Next Hop Type	Next Hop IP
0.0.0.0/0	Virtual Appliance	10.0.2.4 (FW IP)
10.2.0.0/16	Virtual Appliance	10.0.2.4

The route table is then associated with each subnet in the spoke VNet.

Centralized Firewall and Inspection

Deploy **Azure Firewall** in the hub to inspect and control traffic to/from spokes and the internet. All internet-bound traffic should be routed through the firewall using UDRs.

Firewall policies may include:

- Allow only approved outbound ports (80, 443, 22)
- Block known malicious IPs or domains
- Enforce DNS policies
- Log and monitor all traffic for threat intelligence

Sample Azure Firewall Rule:

{

```
"name": "AllowHTTPOutbound",
"priority": 100,
"ruleType": "ApplicationRule",
"action": "Allow",
"sourceAddresses": ["10.1.0.0/16"],
"protocols": [{"protocolType": "Http", "port": 80}],
"targetFqdns": ["*.microsoft.com"]
}
```

Private DNS Integration

When using **Private Endpoints** in spokes, DNS resolution must be handled carefully. Deploy **Azure Private DNS Zones** in the hub and link all spokes to it.

DNS Zone: privatelink.blob.core.windows.net

- Hub: Host DNS resolver (e.g., VM or Azure DNS Forwarder)
- Spokes: Use custom DNS pointing to resolver in hub (e.g., 10.0.4.4)

This enables seamless resolution of private endpoints without public DNS leakage.

Monitoring and Logging

In a hub-and-spoke topology, **centralized monitoring** becomes easier. Deploy **Log Analytics** agents and **Azure Monitor Diagnostic Settings** in the hub to collect:

- NSG Flow Logs
- Firewall logs
- VNet Gateway logs
- Application Gateway WAF logs

Aggregate all logs to a central **Log Analytics Workspace** and use **Kusto Query Language (KQL)** to search across logs.

Sample KQL:

```
AzureDiagnostics

| where ResourceType == "AZUREFIREWALLS"

| where msg_s contains "deny"

| project TimeGenerated, msg_s, src_ip_s, dest_ip_s, protocol_s
```

Automation with Bicep

Provisioning a hub-and-spoke topology manually is error-prone. Use **Bicep** or **Terraform** to automate the entire setup.

Example Bicep snippet for VNet Peering:

```
resource vnetPeering 'Microsoft.Network/virtualNetworks/virtualNetworkPeerings@2022-01-01' = {
```

```
name: 'SpokeToHub'
parent: spokeVnet
properties: {
remoteVirtualNetwork: {
id: hubVnet.id
}
allowVirtualNetworkAccess: true
allowForwardedTraffic: true
}
}
```

Use parameters and modules to create reusable templates for new spokes.

Real-World Scenario: Enterprise Deployment

A multinational organization deploys a hub-and-spoke network as follows:

- **Hub Region (East US)**: Contains Azure Firewall, Bastion, DNS, and ExpressRoute gateway
- **Spokes**: One per business unit (Finance, HR, Engineering)
- **Each spoke VNet**: Hosts isolated workloads with UDRs pointing to the firewall

- **Firewall logs and NSG flows:** Streamed to Sentinel for threat analysis
- **Policies:** Enforced using Azure Policy and Initiative definitions

This model enables secure, auditable communication, scalable application hosting, and centralized control—all while meeting compliance mandates like ISO and SOC 2.

Summary

Hub-and-spoke topology is a cornerstone design for building secure, scalable, and manageable Azure networks. It simplifies connectivity, enforces consistent security policies, centralizes services, and supports effective cost control. By combining VNet peering, UDRs, firewalls, NSGs, and monitoring, organizations can adopt a modular network strategy that aligns with Zero Trust principles and scales effortlessly with growing cloud needs. As workloads and teams grow, the hub-and-spoke model remains flexible, repeatable, and resilient—making it an essential pattern in any enterprise-grade Azure deployment.

Implementing Virtual WAN

As organizations scale their cloud environments, managing connectivity across distributed branches, remote users, on-premises networks, and Azure resources becomes increasingly complex. **Azure Virtual WAN (vWAN)** offers a unified, global, and scalable architecture designed to simplify and optimize large-scale network connectivity. It integrates SD-WAN, VPN, ExpressRoute, and Azure-native connectivity into a single managed hub-and-spoke model, delivering high availability, centralized routing, and streamlined network operations.

In this section, we'll explore the architecture, deployment, configuration, and optimization of Azure Virtual WAN. You'll learn how to implement vWAN to connect branches, users, and cloud workloads across multiple regions securely and efficiently.

What Is Azure Virtual WAN?

Azure Virtual WAN is a **networking service that provides optimized and automated branch connectivity** through Microsoft's global backbone. It combines various networking capabilities into a single unified platform, including:

- **Site-to-site (S2S) VPN**
- **Point-to-site (P2S) VPN**
- **ExpressRoute**
- **User VPN**
- **Azure Firewall Manager integration**
- **Transit routing and hub-to-hub peering**

At the core of Azure vWAN is the **Virtual Hub**, a managed virtual network that serves as a central connection point for your sites and VNets.

Key Benefits of Virtual WAN

- **Global scalability**: Easily scale across regions with Microsoft's global network

- **Centralized security**: Integration with Azure Firewall and third-party security providers
- **Simplicity**: Managed service that reduces configuration and maintenance burden
- **Optimized routing**: Automatic propagation of routes between branches, VNets, and gateways
- **Unified management**: Centralized view and control of all connectivity

---

Core Components

Azure Virtual WAN consists of the following primary components:

- **Virtual WAN Resource**: The overarching resource that holds all vWAN elements
- **Virtual Hubs**: Regional, managed hubs that connect VNets, branches, users
- **Hub Virtual Network Connections**: Connect VNets to hubs
- **Site-to-Site VPN Gateways**: Connect on-premises locations
- **Point-to-Site VPN Gateways**: Secure remote user access
- **ExpressRoute Gateways**: High-performance private connectivity

- **Azure Firewall**: Optional, centrally managed network security

Each hub is connected via Microsoft's backbone, allowing for **hub-to-hub** transit with low latency and high performance.

Creating a Virtual WAN

Azure Portal Steps:

1. Navigate to **Create a resource** > **Networking** > **Virtual WAN**
2. Enter a name, region, and resource group
3. Choose subscription and enable or disable **Branch-to-branch traffic**
4. Review and create the resource

Azure CLI:

```
az network vwan create \

—name MyVirtualWAN \

—resource-group MyResourceGroup \

—location eastus \

—type Standard
```

This creates a virtual WAN container. Next, you'll deploy a **Virtual Hub** in the region you need.

Creating a Virtual Hub

Each Virtual Hub is tied to a specific Azure region and acts as the core of your vWAN topology.

az network vhub create \

—name EastHub \

—resource-group MyResourceGroup \

—vwan MyVirtualWAN \

—address-prefix 10.0.0.0/24 \

—location eastus

Once created, the hub can host gateways and connections.

Connecting VNets to Virtual WAN

Instead of traditional VNet peering, vWAN uses **Hub Virtual Network Connections** to connect VNets to hubs. These connections support **transitive routing** automatically.

az network vhub connection create \

—name VNetConnection1 \

—resource-group MyResourceGroup \

—vhub-name EastHub \

—remote-vnet MySpokeVNetID \

—internet-security true

Setting—internet-security to true enables routing through Azure Firewall in the hub if deployed.

Site-to-Site VPN Configuration

You can connect on-premises locations using standard VPN appliances or SD-WAN devices.

```
az network vpn-site create \
—name HQ-VPN \
—resource-group MyResourceGroup \
—virtual-wan MyVirtualWAN \
—location eastus \
—ip-address 40.112.123.45 \
—asn 65010 \
—device-model Cisco-ASR \
—link-speed 100
az network vpn-site-link-connection create \
—name HQLink \
—resource-group MyResourceGroup \
—hub-name EastHub \
—vpn-site HQ-VPN \
—internet-security true
```

This links your on-prem site to the Azure hub securely and enables internet breakout if required.

Point-to-Site (P2S) VPN for Remote Users

vWAN supports user-level VPN connections using certificates, Azure AD, or RADIUS for authentication.

Steps:

1. Upload root certificates
2. Configure VPN Gateway in the Virtual Hub
3. Distribute VPN client profiles to users

Example P2S gateway creation:

```
az network vhub p2s-vpn-gateway create \

—name P2SGateway \

—resource-group MyResourceGroup \

—vhub-name EastHub \

—vpn-server-configuration MyVPNConfig \

—scale-unit 1
```

Remote users can now securely connect to Azure using the VPN client.

ExpressRoute Integration

vWAN supports **ExpressRoute circuits**, enabling high-bandwidth, private connectivity from your data centers to Azure. The circuits are terminated into Virtual Hubs and propagated automatically.

az network express-route-gateway create \

—name ERGateway \

—resource-group MyResourceGroup \

—vhub-name EastHub \

—scale-units 2

Once connected, ExpressRoute routes are advertised to all VNets attached to the same hub, providing seamless and private connectivity.

Azure Firewall Integration

To enable centralized inspection and logging, deploy **Azure Firewall** in the Virtual Hub.

az network firewall create \

—name vHubFirewall \

—resource-group MyResourceGroup \

—location eastus \

—sku AZFW_VNet

az network firewall policy create \

—name CentralPolicy \

—resource-group MyResourceGroup \

—rule-collection-group-name DefaultRuleGroup

Associate the firewall policy and ensure routing is updated for all hub-connected VNets to flow traffic through the firewall.

Routing and Segmentation

One of the biggest advantages of vWAN is **automated route propagation**. You don't need to manually create UDRs between VNets or branches.

vWAN handles:

- Propagation of on-prem routes to all connected VNets
- Sharing of routes between VNets via the hub
- Support for custom route tables and policies

You can also create **custom route tables** in the hub to implement segmentation or apply specific security policies.

Monitoring and Diagnostics

Use **Azure Monitor**, **Log Analytics**, and **Network Watcher** to observe:

- VPN tunnel status and throughput
- Firewall rule hits
- P2S user sessions
- Route propagation

Sample KQL query:

AzureDiagnostics

| where Category == "AzureFirewallNetworkRule"

| summarize count() by msg_s, SourceIP_s, DestinationIP_s, Protocol_s

Enable diagnostic settings at the Virtual WAN, Virtual Hub, and Firewall level to export logs for centralized analysis.

Real-World Use Case: Global Enterprise

A multinational company with 20 branch offices, 5 data centers, and 10 Azure VNets implements vWAN as follows:

- Deploys **Virtual WAN** with hubs in East US, West Europe, Southeast Asia
- Connects branches via site-to-site VPN into the nearest regional hub
- Enables ExpressRoute for core data centers
- Uses Azure AD for P2S VPN to support remote users globally
- All VNets connect to the hub for shared security and services
- Azure Firewall inspects and logs all outbound traffic

The result: reduced latency, simplified configuration, centralized governance, and a consistent network experience for users across the globe.

Best Practices

- Deploy Virtual Hubs in each major region where workloads or branches exist
- Use Azure Firewall or third-party security appliances in each hub
- Segment traffic using custom route tables
- Minimize the number of VNets per hub to maintain performance
- Regularly review route propagation and firewall logs
- Use Infrastructure as Code (e.g., Bicep, Terraform) to maintain repeatable deployments

---

Summary

Azure Virtual WAN is a powerful solution for enterprises seeking to streamline global network connectivity. It simplifies complex architectures by combining multiple connectivity options into a unified framework. By leveraging vWAN's automated routing, built-in scalability, and integration with Azure Firewall and monitoring tools, you can build a high-performance, secure, and manageable global network backbone.

Implementing Virtual WAN allows organizations to transition away from fragmented VPN topologies, enhance security posture, and centralize operations without sacrificing agility. As workloads and user locations expand, vWAN offers the agility and control needed to operate at enterprise scale with confidence.

Multi-Region Network Architectures

As cloud adoption scales, many enterprises are no longer limited to a single region. Whether to meet performance goals, comply with regulatory requirements, provide disaster recovery, or support global user bases, deploying across multiple Azure regions is now a standard architectural strategy. However, managing connectivity, routing, and security across regions introduces additional complexity. Designing an efficient **multi-region network architecture** is key to ensuring resilience, scalability, and optimized performance.

This section delves into the core considerations, design patterns, connectivity options, routing strategies, security, and monitoring practices that underpin successful multi-region network deployments in Azure.

Why Multi-Region Architectures Matter

Deploying across multiple Azure regions offers:

- **High availability and disaster recovery**: Critical workloads remain available even if a single region fails.
- **Compliance**: Local data residency laws require data to stay within specific geographic boundaries.
- **Performance**: Serving users from their nearest region reduces latency.
- **Load distribution**: Traffic can be balanced between regions to avoid overload.
- **Scalability**: Applications can horizontally scale beyond the limits of a single region.

Despite these benefits, proper planning is crucial to address the networking and security challenges that come with multi-region design.

Core Design Principles

1. **Centralized Governance, Decentralized Execution**: Keep policy, security, and observability centralized while allowing each region to operate independently.
2. **Global Connectivity with Regional Isolation**: Ensure inter-region connectivity without exposing regions unnecessarily.
3. **Consistent Network Topology**: Use the same structure across all regions to simplify management.
4. **Use Azure's Backbone**: Always leverage Microsoft's private backbone for inter-region communication.

Common Multi-Region Network Topologies

1. Hub-and-Spoke Per Region

Each region has its own **hub** and **spokes**, connected to local workloads. Hubs are peered **regionally** and **globally** using VNet peering or **Virtual WAN**.

- Pros:

○ Isolates faults to a region

○ Supports compliance and regulatory zones

- Cons:

  - Requires route control and firewall planning across regions

2. Global Hub-and-Spoke via Virtual WAN

Use **Azure Virtual WAN** with multiple **virtual hubs** deployed in each target region. Microsoft's backbone manages global connectivity and routing.

- Pros:
  - Managed connectivity
  - Automatic route propagation
- Cons:
  - Higher cost
  - Limited customization compared to traditional VNets

3. Single Global Hub

One central hub (in a region like East US or West Europe) serves all spokes globally. All traffic traverses this hub.

- Pros:
  - Simpler to manage
- Cons:
  - Latency issues for remote users
  - Bottleneck risk if hub fails

VNet Peering Across Regions

Global VNet Peering allows VNets in different Azure regions to communicate over Azure's backbone with low latency.

az network vnet peering create \

—name EastUS-to-WestEU \

—resource-group EastRG \

—vnet-name EastVNet \

—remote-vnet /subscriptions/xxx/resourceGroups/WestRG/providers/Microsoft.Network/virtualNetworks/WestVNet \

—allow-vnet-access \

—allow-forwarded-traffic

Considerations:

- Peering is transitive only via a firewall or gateway.
- Bandwidth charges apply for inter-region data transfer.
- NSG rules still apply to peered traffic.

Routing Strategies for Multi-Region Networks

Routing must account for cross-region traffic, failover paths, and inspection zones.

1. Static UDRs

In simple deployments, **User-Defined Routes** (UDRs) are configured to direct traffic via specific firewalls or gateways.

Example: Route traffic from Spoke A in Region 1 to Spoke B in Region 2 via the firewall in Region 1.

Prefix	Next Hop Type	Next Hop IP
10.20.0.0/16	Virtual Appliance	10.1.2.4 (FW IP)

2. Route Server

Use **Azure Route Server** in each hub to dynamically learn and distribute routes using BGP. Works well with NVAs and simplifies route propagation across spokes.

```
az network routeserver create \

—name EastRouteServer \

—resource-group EastRG \

—location eastus \

—hosted-subnet RouteServerSubnet \

—public-ip-address EastRouteServerIP
```

3. Virtual WAN Route Propagation

With vWAN, you configure custom route tables per hub and define **propagation rules** and **associations** to control which hubs or VNets receive certain routes.

Cross-Region Failover and DR

Designing for DR requires seamless routing in case a region goes down.

Active-Active

- Both regions are fully operational.
- Traffic is distributed based on geographic proximity or availability.

Tools: Azure Front Door, Traffic Manager, DNS Failover

Active-Passive

- Primary region handles traffic; secondary region is on standby.
- DNS or route-level failover required.

Failover Steps:

1. Update DNS (or let Traffic Manager redirect)
2. Flip UDRs or BGP paths to point to secondary region
3. Rehydrate replicated services (SQL, Storage, VMs)

Automated failover via Azure Site Recovery (ASR) or Logic Apps is recommended.

Security Considerations

Securing a multi-region network requires consistent security enforcement, visibility, and auditing.

- **Firewall per hub**: Deploy **Azure Firewall** in each hub for regional traffic control.
- **Policy enforcement**: Use **Azure Policy** to apply NSG, route, and private endpoint rules across regions.
- **Private Link**: Use Private Endpoints for cross-region service consumption without public exposure.
- **Sentinel**: Centralize threat detection across all regions.

Example: Enforce Private DNS zone registration for all VNets

```
{
"if": {
"field": "Microsoft.Network/virtualNetworks/enableDnsPrivate"
},
"then": {
"effect": "deny"
}
}
```

Monitoring and Telemetry

Use a **centralized Log Analytics workspace** for all regions or link workspaces into **Azure Monitor** for unified queries.

Cross-region NSG log analysis (KQL):

```
AzureDiagnostics
```

| where Category == "NetworkSecurityGroupFlowEvent"

| where Region_s in ("eastus", "westeurope")

| summarize Count = count() by FlowDirection_s, SourceIP_s, DestinationIP_s, Region_s

Enable diagnostic settings for:

- NSGs
- Firewalls
- Route servers
- ExpressRoute circuits
- Virtual WAN

Set up alerts for anomalies like failed cross-region communications or unexpected route changes.

Automation and Deployment

Use **Infrastructure as Code (IaC)** to manage multi-region infrastructure:

- **Bicep/Terraform**: Modularize each region
- **Azure Blueprints**: Apply consistent compliance and configurations
- **GitHub Actions / Azure DevOps Pipelines**: Automate hub/spoke creation, peering, UDRs, and security

Sample Bicep Template Snippet for Multi-Region Hub:

```
module eastHub './hub.bicep' = {
name: 'eastHub'
params: {
region: 'eastus'
}
}
module westHub './hub.bicep' = {
name: 'westHub'
params: {
region: 'westeurope'
}
}
```

Use parameterization to reuse templates across all geographies.

Real-World Architecture: Retail Chain

A global retail company deploys a multi-region Azure architecture:

- **East US Hub**: Main data center, VPN gateway, SQL servers
- **West Europe Hub**: E-commerce platform, backup storage

- **Southeast Asia Hub**: Customer analytics, regional apps

Each hub has its own firewall, bastion, and monitoring setup. VNets in each region connect to their local hub and communicate cross-region via global peering and UDRs. Azure Front Door is used for global load balancing. Azure Policy enforces private DNS and restricted egress. All diagnostics flow to a centralized Sentinel instance in East US.

This setup provides global availability, localized performance, and centralized governance.

Summary

Multi-region network architectures are essential for modern, resilient cloud environments. Azure provides the tools, patterns, and flexibility to build networks that span continents while maintaining security, performance, and operational control.

By leveraging hub-and-spoke topologies, Virtual WAN, VNet peering, dynamic routing, and centralized security services, you can create a scalable and reliable architecture that meets the demands of global users and applications. The key is to treat regions as semi-autonomous domains, unified under consistent governance and observability, enabling your cloud network to grow intelligently alongside your business.

Integrating Azure Load Balancers

In any scalable and resilient cloud architecture, **load balancing** plays a pivotal role in distributing network traffic efficiently across multiple resources, ensuring high availability and responsiveness. Azure provides several types of load balancers tailored to different layers and use cases, including **Azure Load Balancer**, **Azure Application Gateway**, **Azure Front Door**, and **Traffic Manager**. Each of these services integrates differently into a network design, and understanding how to use them individually and in combination is key to building reliable systems.

This section focuses on integrating **Azure Load Balancer (Layer 4)** into your network infrastructure, how it complements higher-layer services, and how it can be used in various network patterns such as internal load balancing, hybrid connectivity, and global deployments.

Understanding Azure Load Balancer

Azure Load Balancer operates at **OSI Layer 4 (TCP/UDP)** and is designed for high-performance, ultra-low-latency, and high-throughput workloads.

Key characteristics:

- Supports **inbound and outbound NAT**
- Two SKUs: **Basic** and **Standard**
- **Public** and **Internal** configurations
- Highly available and zone-redundant
- Integration with **Virtual Machine Scale Sets (VMSS)**
- Health probes to monitor backend availability
- Works in tandem with **Network Security Groups (NSGs)** and **User-Defined Routes (UDRs)**

Load Balancer Types and Use Cases

Type	Use Case
Public Load Balancer	Inbound internet access to Azure resources
Internal Load Balancer	Load balancing within a VNet
Gateway Load Balancer	Service chaining with NVAs (e.g., firewalls)

Deploying a Public Load Balancer

A **Public Load Balancer** provides internet access to backend resources such as web servers or APIs. It is associated with a **public IP address** and balances inbound connections.

Basic Deployment Example:

az network lb create \

—name MyPublicLB \

—resource-group MyResourceGroup \

—sku Standard \

—frontend-ip-name LoadBalancerFrontEnd \

—backend-pool-name LoadBalancerBackEnd \

—public-ip-address MyPublicIP

Next, configure the health probe:

az network lb probe create \

—resource-group MyResourceGroup \

—lb-name MyPublicLB \

—name HttpProbe \

—protocol Http \

—port 80 \

—path /

And add a load balancing rule:

az network lb rule create \

—resource-group MyResourceGroup \

—lb-name MyPublicLB \

—name HttpRule \

—protocol Tcp \

—frontend-port 80 \

—backend-port 80 \

—frontend-ip-name LoadBalancerFrontEnd \

—backend-pool-name LoadBalancerBackEnd \

—probe-name HttpProbe

Attach your VMs or VM scale sets to the backend pool, ensuring NSGs permit inbound traffic.

Deploying an Internal Load Balancer (ILB)

An **Internal Load Balancer** is used within VNets to distribute traffic across resources **without exposing them to the internet.**

Typical use cases:

- Load balancing between application tiers (e.g., web → app → DB)
- Private API endpoints
- Hybrid or multi-region service tiers

Deployment Example:

az network lb create \

—name InternalLB \

—resource-group AppRG \

—sku Standard \

—frontend-ip-name InternalFrontEnd \

—backend-pool-name AppPool \

—vnet-name AppVNet \

—subnet AppSubnet \

—private-ip-address 10.10.1.10

Pair this with proper NSG rules and route tables to direct intra-VNet traffic through the ILB.

Gateway Load Balancer

Gateway Load Balancer is a Layer 3 service that simplifies **insertion of network virtual appliances (NVAs)** into your traffic path. It allows seamless service chaining of appliances like firewalls, IDS/IPS, or packet inspection tools.

Key Use Cases:

- Centralized perimeter firewalls
- Intrusion detection and prevention
- Traffic analytics

Integration Flow:

1. Attach Gateway Load Balancer to the backend of a Public Load Balancer
2. The Public Load Balancer frontend receives the traffic
3. Traffic is forwarded through Gateway Load Balancer to the NVA
4. NVA returns traffic to the backend pool

This model supports **transparent inspection** and simplified scaling of third-party security solutions.

Load Balancer SKUs: Basic vs. Standard

Feature	Basic	Standard
Availability Zones	Not supported	Supported
Backend Pool Scaling	Up to 100	Up to 1000
Health Probes	Limited	Enhanced (TCP/HTTP/HTTPS)
NSG Enforcement	Not required	Mandatory
Diagnostics	No integration	Full Azure Monitor support
Cross-region Load Balancing	Not supported	Supported via Global Tier

Recommendation: Always use **Standard SKU** for production due to its feature set, security, and diagnostics.

Outbound Connectivity via Load Balancer

Azure Load Balancer enables **outbound internet access** using **Outbound Rules** or NAT Rules.

To configure outbound connectivity for a VM:

```
az network lb outbound-rule create \

—resource-group MyResourceGroup \

—lb-name MyPublicLB \

—name OutboundInternet \

—protocol All \

—frontend-ip-configs LoadBalancerFrontEnd \

—backend-pool-name LoadBalancerBackEnd
```

This ensures that VMs in the backend pool can access the internet using the Load Balancer's public IP.

High Availability and Redundancy

To achieve redundancy:

- Use **Availability Zones** in your region and place backend instances across zones
- Use **Zone-redundant Load Balancers**
- Set up **health probes** for fast failover detection

- Ensure **backend autoscaling** with VMSS

When designing for **disaster recovery**, deploy **paired region load balancers** and leverage **Azure Front Door** or **Traffic Manager** for failover.

Diagnostics and Monitoring

Enable **diagnostic logs** on Load Balancers to capture metrics and health probe results:

az monitor diagnostic-settings create \

—resource /subscriptions/xxx/resourceGroups/rg/providers/Microsoft.Network/loadBalancers/MyPublicLB \

—name LBDiagnostics \

—workspace MyLogAnalyticsWorkspaceID \

—logs '[{"category": "LoadBalancerAlertEvent", "enabled": true}]'

Monitor:

- Probe status
- Backend availability
- Rule match frequency
- Connection success/failure rates

Sample KQL to identify failed health probes:

AzureDiagnostics

| where Category == "LoadBalancerProbeHealthStatus"

```
| where status_s == "Unhealthy"

| summarize count() by Resource, IP_s, TimeGenerated
```

Hybrid and Multi-Region Integration

In **hybrid scenarios**, use **Internal Load Balancer (ILB)** in conjunction with **VPN Gateways** or **ExpressRoute**. This enables secure access from on-premises to private Azure services without public exposure.

In **multi-region scenarios**, use **Azure Front Door** or **Traffic Manager** for global traffic distribution and pair them with regional Load Balancers for backend handling.

Example Architecture:

- Azure Front Door routes traffic to East US or West Europe based on proximity
- Regional Public Load Balancers forward traffic to web VMs or containers
- ILBs manage traffic between app tiers
- Gateway Load Balancers insert NVAs for inspection

Automation with Bicep

Sample Bicep Template:

```
resource lb 'Microsoft.Network/loadBalancers@2022-01-01' = {

name: 'myStandardLB'

location: resourceGroup().location
```

```
sku: {
name: 'Standard'
}
properties: {
frontendIPConfigurations: [
{
name: 'LoadBalancerFrontEnd'
properties: {
publicIPAddress: {
id: publicIp.id
}
}
}
]
backendAddressPools: [
{
name: 'LoadBalancerBackEnd'
}
]
loadBalancingRules: [
```

```
{
name: 'HttpRule'
properties: {
frontendIPConfiguration: {
id: lb.properties.frontendIPConfigurations[0].id
}
backendAddressPool: {
id: lb.properties.backendAddressPools[0].id
}
protocol: 'Tcp'
frontendPort: 80
backendPort: 80
enableFloatingIP: false
idleTimeoutInMinutes: 4
probe: {
id: probe.id
}
}
}
]
```

```
}
}
```

This can be extended with modules to automate ILBs, health probes, and outbound rules.

Real-World Example: E-Commerce Application

A large e-commerce platform uses Azure Load Balancers as follows:

- **Public Load Balancer**: Handles HTTPS traffic from users and forwards it to Azure Kubernetes Service (AKS)
- **Gateway Load Balancer**: Routes incoming traffic through a Palo Alto firewall NVA
- **Internal Load Balancer**: Balances internal traffic between microservices
- **Regional ILBs**: Used in each region for data tier access
- **Outbound Load Balancer**: Handles internet-bound traffic from compute nodes using NAT

Monitoring is centralized via Log Analytics, and failover is orchestrated using Azure Traffic Manager with weighted routing policies.

Summary

Azure Load Balancer is a fundamental building block for high-performance, reliable, and secure Azure deployments. By understanding how to deploy and integrate public, internal, and gateway load balancers, you can create resilient architectures that scale with business needs. When paired with monitoring, automation, and complementary services like Azure Firewall, Application Gateway, and Front Door, load balancers provide seamless and optimized traffic flow within and across Azure regions.

Design with a focus on fault tolerance, security boundaries, and global reach, and you'll unlock the full potential of load balancing in your cloud-native and hybrid environments.

Chapter 7: Monitoring and Troubleshooting

Azure Network Watcher Tools

Monitoring and troubleshooting are vital components of any robust networking strategy in Azure. As your cloud infrastructure scales, it becomes increasingly important to gain visibility into the health, performance, and behavior of your virtual networks. Azure provides a suite of powerful tools under the **Azure Network Watcher** service, which helps administrators inspect, diagnose, and monitor their network configurations in real-time. In this section, we'll delve deeply into the capabilities of Network Watcher, how to use each tool effectively, and best practices for integrating monitoring into your operational workflows.

What Is Azure Network Watcher?

Azure Network Watcher is a regional service that enables and simplifies network monitoring and diagnostics for IaaS resources in Azure. It allows you to monitor, diagnose, view metrics, and enable or disable logs for resources in a virtual network. You can use it to:

- Monitor network performance
- Diagnose issues using built-in diagnostics
- Visualize the topology of your virtual network
- Verify connectivity between endpoints
- Capture packet traffic for analysis

Network Watcher is not enabled by default in all regions. However, once it's enabled in a region, it can automatically monitor all VMs and networking resources within that region.

Enabling Azure Network Watcher

You can enable Network Watcher either through the Azure Portal, PowerShell, Azure CLI, or ARM templates. Here's how to enable it via the CLI:

�az network watcher configure—locations eastus—resource-group MyResourceGroup—enabled true

�Or via PowerShell:

�Enable-AzNetworkWatcher -Name "NetworkWatcher_eastus" -ResourceGroupName "NetworkWatcherRG"

�Ensure that you enable Network Watcher in every region where you plan to deploy networking resources for full coverage.

Key Features of Azure Network Watcher

Topology

The Topology tool provides a graphical representation of your virtual network, including VNets, subnets, NICs, NSGs, and other resources. It helps you understand how resources are connected and aids in visual troubleshooting.

To access the topology:

1. Go to the Azure Portal
2. Navigate to **Network Watcher > Topology**
3. Select the subscription, resource group, and virtual

network

While the portal visualization is useful, you can also extract topology data via the Azure CLI:

�az network watcher show-topology—location eastus—resource-group MyResourceGroup

�IP Flow Verify

IP Flow Verify checks whether a packet from a specific source IP, destination IP, source port, and destination port is allowed or denied. This is essential when you need to confirm if NSG or route configurations are affecting connectivity.

Example using Azure CLI:

�az network watcher test-ip-flow \

—resource-group MyResourceGroup \

—direction Inbound \

—protocol TCP \

—local 10.0.0.4 \

—remote 192.168.1.1 \

—local-port 80 \

—remote-port 12345 \

—nic MyVMNIC

�This command will output whether the traffic is allowed and which rule is responsible for the decision.

Connection Troubleshoot

This tool performs a connectivity check between two endpoints, such as two VMs or a VM and a web endpoint. It provides latency, packet loss, and hop-by-hop diagnostics.

To troubleshoot from a VM to a URL:

```
az network watcher connection-monitor test-configuration add \
—connection-monitor-name MyMonitor \
—location eastus \
—source-resource MyVMID \
—destination-address www.microsoft.com \
—destination-port 443
```

Packet Capture

Packet Capture lets you capture and inspect traffic to and from a VM for in-depth analysis. This is useful for identifying malicious activity, checking headers, or debugging application behavior.

Here's a simplified version of how to start a packet capture using the CLI:

```
az network watcher packet-capture create \
—name CaptureSession1 \
—resource-group MyResourceGroup \
—vm MyVM \
```

—storage-account mystorageaccount \

—file-path mycontainer/capture1.cap

�After capturing, you can download the .cap file and analyze it using Wireshark or a similar tool.

NSG Flow Logs

Flow logs provide information about ingress and egress IP traffic through an NSG. You can use these logs to analyze traffic patterns, spot anomalies, and audit access controls.

Enabling NSG flow logs:

1. Go to **Network Watcher > NSG Flow Logs**
2. Choose the NSG to monitor
3. Set the version and retention
4. Select a storage account for the logs

Alternatively, via CLI:

�az network watcher flow-log configure \

—resource-group MyResourceGroup \

—nsg MyNSG \

—enabled true \

—retention 7 \

—storage-account mystorageaccount

�Logs are stored in JSON format and can be integrated with Azure Monitor or third-party SIEM tools.

Integration with Azure Monitor

Azure Network Watcher can forward metrics and logs to Azure Monitor, enabling you to set up alerts, dashboards, and long-term storage. Common alerts include:

- Unusual increases in dropped packets
- Latency spikes between services
- Unexpected traffic sources

To configure diagnostics for forwarding:

```
az monitor diagnostic-settings create \
—resource MyNetworkResourceID \
—name "MyDiagSettings" \
—workspace MyLogAnalyticsWorkspaceID \
—logs
'[{"category":"NetworkSecurityGroupFlowEvent","enabled":true}]'
```

Best Practices for Using Network Watcher

- **Enable in all regions:** Don't assume your region has Network Watcher enabled—check and enable explicitly.
- **Automate with templates:** Use ARM or Bicep templates to ensure consistent configuration across environments.
- **Use tags and naming conventions:** To streamline topology views and diagnostics.

- **Regularly review flow logs:** Integrate with SIEM systems and set up alerts for unexpected patterns.
- **Capture packets during off-peak hours:** To avoid performance degradation on production VMs.
- **Limit packet capture duration and scope:** Define specific filters to narrow down relevant traffic.

Troubleshooting Common Scenarios

Scenario: VM Cannot Reach Internet

Checklist:

- Is the VM in a subnet with a valid route to the internet?
- Is there a public IP assigned?
- Are NSGs blocking outbound traffic?
- Use **IP Flow Verify** to check port 443 or 80.
- Use **Connection Troubleshoot** to validate reachability.

Scenario: Intermittent VM-to-VM Connectivity

Checklist:

- Use **Packet Capture** to inspect failed connections.
- Validate NSG flow logs for dropped traffic.
- Check for conflicting UDRs or peering configurations.

- Use **Topology** to ensure correct associations.

Cost Considerations

Most Network Watcher features are free or have nominal costs. However, packet captures, diagnostics storage, and flow logs may incur charges for:

- Storage
- Data processing
- Network bandwidth (if data is sent across regions)

Be sure to set retention policies and clean up old resources to minimize cost.

Azure Network Watcher is a foundational component of maintaining operational excellence in cloud networking. Whether you're managing a handful of virtual networks or a complex multi-region architecture, Network Watcher provides the tools necessary to observe, troubleshoot, and optimize your connectivity and security posture. Proper use of its capabilities can significantly reduce downtime, accelerate root cause analysis, and improve the overall health of your Azure infrastructure.

Diagnosing Connectivity Issues

Diagnosing network connectivity issues in Azure can be a complex task, especially as infrastructures scale and become more distributed. Whether it's a misconfigured NSG, a broken route, or a failed VPN tunnel, connectivity issues can manifest in numerous ways. In this section, we'll explore the methods and tools you can use to systematically diagnose, isolate, and resolve such issues. We'll examine native Azure diagnostics, logical troubleshooting steps, common failure scenarios, and how to approach debugging in both test and production environments.

Understanding the Layers of Azure Networking

Before jumping into diagnostics, it's critical to understand the different layers where connectivity can break down. Issues may originate at:

- **Network Interface (NIC) configuration**
- **Virtual Network/Subnet boundaries**
- **Network Security Groups (NSGs)**
- **Route Tables (UDRs)**
- **Application Security Groups (ASGs)**
- **Load balancers and NAT rules**
- **VPN or ExpressRoute gateways**
- **DNS misconfigurations**
- **Application-level restrictions or timeouts**

By approaching diagnostics from the bottom up (infrastructure to application) or top down (user experience to backend systems), you can identify the root cause more effectively.

Step-by-Step Troubleshooting Workflow

1. Confirm the Scope of the Issue

Begin by asking the right questions:

- Is this issue affecting one VM or multiple?
- Is it localized to a specific region, VNet, or subnet?
- Is it a new deployment or something that was previously working?
- Are other services able to communicate with the affected endpoint?

A clear understanding of the scope can drastically narrow down potential causes.

2. Ping and TraceRoute

From the affected VM, use basic tools like ping and tracert (or traceroute on Linux) to test external and internal connectivity:

ping 10.0.1.4

tracert www.microsoft.com

Keep in mind that ICMP might be blocked by default in NSGs or the OS firewall, so the failure of ping doesn't necessarily indicate an issue unless it's explicitly permitted.

3. Check NSGs and ASGs

Network Security Groups are one of the most common culprits for blocked connectivity. Each VM's NIC and subnet can be associated with NSGs. Ensure that the correct inbound and outbound rules are applied.

Use this CLI command to list effective NSG rules:

az network nic list-effective-nsg—name MyVMNIC—resource-group MyRG

If ASGs are in use, verify that the VM is part of the correct group and that the ASG rules are not overly restrictive.

4. Inspect UDRs and System Routes

User Defined Routes can override default system routes and cause unintended network behavior, especially if next hops are misconfigured.

List effective routes for a VM:

az network nic show-effective-route-table—name MyVMNIC—resource-group MyRG

Look for:

- Blackhole routes
- Unexpected next hop types (e.g., Virtual Appliance instead of Internet)
- Missing system routes for VNet-to-VNet or peered networks

5. Diagnose DNS Issues

Connectivity problems are sometimes caused by name resolution failures. Ensure the correct DNS servers are configured at the VNet or NIC level. You can test name resolution using:

nslookup myapp.internal.cloudapp.net

Azure-provided DNS (168.63.129.16) is default unless overridden. Custom DNS servers should be reachable and properly configured to resolve internal and external names.

6. Use Connection Troubleshoot

Network Watcher's Connection Troubleshoot feature allows you to simulate a connection between a source and destination. It helps you test port accessibility and diagnose NSG or UDR-related issues.

az network watcher connection-monitor test-configuration add \

—connection-monitor-name MyMonitor \

—location eastus \

—source-resource /subscriptions/.../resourceGroups/MyRG/providers/Microsoft.Compute/virtualMachines/MyVM \

—destination-address 10.1.0.5 \

—destination-port 1433

This provides detailed output including:

- Success/failure status
- Latency

- Hop-by-hop path

7. Use IP Flow Verify

This tool checks whether traffic between source and destination is allowed based on NSG rules.

az network watcher test-ip-flow \

—resource-group MyRG \

—direction Outbound \

—protocol TCP \

—local 10.0.0.4 \

—remote 52.174.112.53 \

—local-port 443 \

—remote-port 443 \

—nic MyNIC

It will indicate whether the traffic is allowed or denied and the rule that applies.

8. Packet Captures

When all else fails, packet capture is your go-to for deep analysis. You can capture traffic to and from a VM and download the .cap file for inspection with tools like Wireshark.

Start a packet capture:

az network watcher packet-capture create \

—name Capture1 \

—resource-group MyRG \

—vm MyVM \

—storage-account mystorageacct \

—file-path mycontainer/session1.cap

Use filters to narrow traffic (e.g., only HTTP or DNS). Keep captures short to reduce VM performance impact.

Troubleshooting Common Scenarios

Scenario 1: Application Works Locally but Not from Another VM

Checklist:

- Confirm application is listening on the correct IP/port using netstat -an or ss -tuln
- Check that the NSG allows inbound traffic to the application port
- Use IP Flow Verify to confirm packet permission
- Test with Connection Troubleshoot from the other VM

Scenario 2: VM Can't Reach Internet

Checklist:

- Is the VM in a subnet with a route to Internet?
- Does it have a public IP or go through a NAT gateway?
- Are outbound NSG rules allowing internet ports (80, 443)?
- Is DNS working properly?

Scenario 3: Intermittent VM-to-VM Communication

Checklist:

- Packet loss can be a sign of:
  - Overloaded NIC or host
  - Misconfigured load balancer
  - Intermittent DNS resolution issues
- Use continuous ping and packet capture to trace root cause

Scenario 4: VPN Site-to-Site Tunnel Down

Checklist:

- Verify both on-prem and Azure VPN device status
- Use Network Watcher VPN diagnostics
- Check shared keys and IPSEC/IKE settings
- Examine logs from on-prem firewall or router

- Confirm Azure gateway SKU supports required configuration

Scenario 5: Load Balancer Not Routing Traffic

Checklist:

- Is the backend pool healthy?
- Are health probes configured correctly?
- Are NSG rules allowing inbound/outbound to backend pool?
- Use Connection Troubleshoot to validate routing path

Automation for Diagnostics

For repeatable environments, automation can be key to proactive diagnostics. You can script all the above steps using Azure CLI, PowerShell, or Bicep. For example, here's a script to test NSG flow and route table for all NICs in a resource group:

for nic in $(az network nic list—query "[].name" -o tsv); do

echo "Checking $nic..."

az network nic list-effective-nsg—name $nic—resource-group MyRG

az network nic show-effective-route-table—name $nic—resource-group MyRG

done

This gives quick visibility into potential NSG or routing issues across a deployment.

Best Practices

- **Tag environments** (e.g., env:prod) to quickly locate affected resources
- **Enable diagnostics and logging** at the start of a project
- **Maintain documentation** for custom routes and NSGs
- **Isolate traffic** using subnets and route tables for cleaner troubleshooting
- **Use service health alerts** for regional or platform outages
- **Schedule routine connection tests** for mission-critical services

Conclusion

Diagnosing connectivity issues in Azure involves a methodical approach—starting with understanding the architecture and moving through layers of the network stack. By leveraging Azure-native tools like Network Watcher, IP Flow Verify, Connection Troubleshoot, and packet capture, you can detect and resolve most issues efficiently. Whether the challenge lies in misconfigured NSGs, faulty DNS resolution, or failed VPN connections, Azure provides the insights and control needed to maintain a healthy and responsive cloud network.

Metrics, Logs, and Alerts

In any cloud-based architecture, real-time observability is a cornerstone of reliability, performance, and security. Azure provides an extensive suite of tools to monitor and analyze metrics, logs, and set alerts for networking resources, helping administrators identify anomalies before they escalate into critical incidents. This section delves into how to collect, interpret, and act on metrics and logs across Azure networking components, and how to configure alerts that enable proactive monitoring.

The Three Pillars of Observability

Azure aligns with the industry-standard approach to observability, focusing on:

- **Metrics**: Numeric data representing system behavior over time (e.g., CPU usage, data in/out).
- **Logs**: Records of discrete events, operations, or status changes (e.g., NSG flow logs, packet capture).
- **Alerts**: Triggered notifications based on defined conditions from metrics or logs.

These components work together to help teams understand and manage the performance and security of their virtual networks and associated services.

Azure Monitor Overview

Azure Monitor is the unified platform for collecting and analyzing telemetry data from Azure resources. It encompasses multiple services, including:

- **Azure Metrics Explorer** for visualizing performance
- **Log Analytics** for querying logs
- **Action Groups** for notifications
- **Alerts** for real-time condition monitoring

Network-specific monitoring in Azure includes:

- NSG Flow Logs
- Azure Firewall Logs
- Application Gateway Access and Performance Logs
- ExpressRoute and VPN Gateway Metrics
- Load Balancer Health Metrics
- Network Watcher Tools

Collecting Metrics for Azure Network Resources

Metrics are available for nearly every network component and are useful for understanding trends and capacity planning.

Examples of Available Metrics:

Resource	Metric	Use Case
Virtual Network	Bytes Sent/Received	Track traffic trends over time
Azure Firewall	Throughput, SNAT Port Utilization	Detect bottlenecks or exhausted resources
Application Gateway	Current Connections, Failed Requests	Monitor load and failure patterns
VPN Gateway	Tunnel Up/Down, P2S Connection Count	Check tunnel health and user access
Load Balancer	Data Path Availability, Probe Count	Ensure backend availability

To list available metrics via CLI:

```
az monitor metrics list-definitions \

—resource
/subscriptions/<sub-id>/resourceGroups/<rg>/providers/
Microsoft.Network/virtualNetworks/<vnet-name>
```

To view metrics:

```
az monitor metrics list \

—resource <resource-id> \

—metric "BytesSent" \

—interval PT1H \

—aggregation Total
```

Logging for Diagnostics and Audit

Logs provide detailed insight into what's happening in your network at the packet, request, or policy enforcement level.

NSG Flow Logs

NSG flow logs capture information about IP traffic flowing through an NSG. These logs are stored in a JSON format and include:

- Source and destination IP
- Source and destination port
- Protocol
- Action (Allow/Deny)
- Flow state (Initiated, Terminated)

To enable flow logs:

```
az network watcher flow-log configure \
—resource-group MyResourceGroup \
—nsg MyNSG \
—enabled true \
—retention 30 \
—storage-account mystorageaccount \
—format JSON
```

The logs can be queried using Kusto Query Language (KQL) in Log Analytics:

```
AzureDiagnostics

| where Category == "NetworkSecurityGroupFlowEvent"

| where action_s == "Deny"

| summarize count() by src_ip_s, dest_ip_s
```

Azure Firewall Logs

Firewall diagnostics include both application and network rule matches and are critical for understanding permitted and blocked traffic.

Enable logging via Diagnostic Settings:

```
az monitor diagnostic-settings create \

—resource <firewall-resource-id> \

—name "FirewallLogs" \

—workspace <log-analytics-id> \

—logs '[{"category":"AzureFirewallApplicationRule","enabled":true},
{"category":"AzureFirewallNetworkRule","enabled":true}]'
```

Sample query:

```
AzureDiagnostics

| where ResourceType == "AZUREFIREWALLS"

| where msg_s contains "Deny"
```

| project TimeGenerated, msg_s, src_ip_s, dest_ip_s, protocol_s

Application Gateway Logs

Includes:

- Access logs
- Performance logs
- Firewall logs (if WAF is enabled)

Common use cases:

- Investigating slow responses
- Identifying blocked requests
- Tracing user paths through applications

Enable diagnostics as with the firewall, then use KQL to query logs.

Creating Actionable Alerts

Azure Alerts allow you to define rules that monitor metrics or logs and notify responsible parties or trigger automated remediation.

Creating a Metric Alert

For example, to create an alert for high throughput on a firewall:

az monitor metrics alert create \

—name HighFirewallThroughput \

—resource-group MyResourceGroup \

```
—scopes
/subscriptions/<sub-id>/resourceGroups/<rg>/providers/
Microsoft.Network/azureFirewalls/MyFirewall \

—condition "avg AzureFirewallThroughput > 50000000" \

—description "High throughput alert on firewall" \

—action-group MyActionGroup
```

Creating a Log-Based Alert

You might want to trigger an alert when more than 100 denied NSG connections occur in 5 minutes:

```
AzureDiagnostics

| where Category == "NetworkSecurityGroupFlowEvent"

| where action_s == "Deny"

| summarize count() by bin(TimeGenerated, 5m)
```

Then configure an alert rule on this query using the Azure Portal or ARM templates.

Action Groups

An action group defines how alerts are delivered—via email, webhook, SMS, logic app, Azure Functions, etc.

Example CLI command:

```
az monitor action-group create \

—resource-group MyRG \
```

—name MyActionGroup \

—short-name "NetMon" \

—email-receiver name="NetOpsTeam" email="netops@company.com"

Dashboards and Visualization

To make metrics and logs actionable, it's helpful to visualize them in dashboards. Azure offers two main tools:

- **Azure Dashboards**: Custom views using metrics charts, logs tables, and tiles.
- **Workbooks**: More flexible and interactive dashboards built on KQL queries.

Example: Create a workbook that shows:

- Top 10 blocked source IPs (from NSG logs)
- VPN Gateway tunnel status over time
- Application Gateway latency metrics

You can export dashboards or pin specific tiles to your Azure Portal home for quick visibility.

Long-Term Archiving and Compliance

Logs and metrics can be retained for years in Log Analytics or exported to:

- Azure Blob Storage (for cold storage)

- Event Hubs (for SIEM integration)
- Sentinel (for security analytics)

To archive to Blob Storage:

```
az monitor diagnostic-settings create \
—resource <resource-id> \
—name ArchiveLogs \
—storage-account <storage-id> \
—logs '[{"category":"AllLogs","enabled":true}]'
```

Ensure compliance with organizational retention policies by setting appropriate lifecycle rules.

Best Practices

- **Enable diagnostics early**: Logging after an incident is too late.
- **Define baselines**: Understand what "normal" looks like in your network.
- **Use tags and naming conventions**: Helps in filtering and organizing logs.
- **Set up alert suppression and throttling**: To avoid alert fatigue.
- **Review alerts regularly**: Retire unused ones and fine-tune noisy conditions.

- **Centralize monitoring**: Use Log Analytics workspaces strategically for shared visibility.

Summary

Azure's networking telemetry ecosystem offers powerful capabilities to monitor performance, ensure uptime, and detect security incidents. By collecting meaningful **metrics**, analyzing detailed **logs**, and configuring smart **alerts**, administrators can maintain full visibility and control over their virtual networks. Whether it's bandwidth saturation, unusual connection patterns, or packet loss, these tools enable proactive rather than reactive network management. A consistent and integrated observability strategy built on Azure Monitor helps keep infrastructure secure, performant, and resilient at scale.

Best Practices for Network Health Checks

Maintaining the health of your Azure network infrastructure is essential for ensuring reliability, performance, and security. Regular network health checks are critical to identifying and addressing potential issues before they affect end users or system performance. In this section, we will explore the best practices and strategies for performing comprehensive health checks on your network in Azure. We'll cover tools, methodologies, and recurring processes for monitoring the state of your network infrastructure, as well as how to implement proactive health checks to prevent downtime or performance degradation.

The Importance of Network Health Checks

Network health checks are essential for maintaining a high-performing, secure, and reliable cloud environment. By implementing a robust health check routine, administrators can:

- Detect performance bottlenecks before they impact users
- Identify configuration issues (e.g., misconfigured NSGs, failed routes)
- Monitor and optimize resource utilization
- Ensure compliance with organizational security policies
- Track key performance indicators (KPIs) over time for proactive maintenance

Components of Network Health Checks

A comprehensive network health check typically includes the following components:

- **Connectivity Checks**: Verifying that network traffic can flow between required endpoints (e.g., VMs, load balancers, external services).
- **Security Health**: Checking that NSGs, firewalls, and other security configurations are correctly implemented and not overly restrictive.
- **Performance Health**: Ensuring that network resources (e.g., VPNs, load balancers, firewalls) are performing optimally and within expected thresholds.
- **Configuration Integrity**: Verifying that all configuration settings (e.g., routes, peerings) are accurate and aligned with the network design.

Tools for Network Health Checks

Azure offers several built-in tools that can be used to conduct network health checks. These tools help to automate the monitoring process, reducing manual intervention and enabling a more proactive approach to network management.

Azure Network Watcher

Azure Network Watcher provides a comprehensive suite of monitoring and diagnostics tools that are essential for regular network health checks. Key features include:

- **Topology**: Visualize the layout of your virtual networks, including resources like VNets, subnets, and network interfaces (NICs).

- **IP Flow Verify**: Test whether traffic between specific source and destination IPs is allowed based on NSG and route table settings.

- **Connection Troubleshoot**: Simulate a connection between two endpoints to check connectivity.

- **Packet Capture**: Capture and analyze packets between VMs to identify potential network-related issues.

- **NSG Flow Logs**: Capture all traffic passing through a Network Security Group to analyze which connections are being allowed or denied.

Using **Network Watcher** for regular checks ensures that you have visibility into the state of your network and can quickly identify any issues that might arise.

Azure Monitor

Azure Monitor is a platform service that provides full-stack monitoring and diagnostic capabilities. It includes:

- **Metrics**: Collects performance data from your network resources, including throughput, traffic, and latency.
- **Logs**: Provides detailed logs from Azure services such as Azure Firewall, Application Gateway, and Network Security Groups.
- **Alerts**: Configures custom alerts to notify you of critical network health issues, such as high latency, packet loss, or unusually high traffic patterns.
- **Workbooks**: Visualize your network health metrics in customizable dashboards for easy monitoring and decision-making.

By leveraging **Azure Monitor**, you can create custom dashboards to track the health of your network infrastructure and set up automatic alerts for performance degradation or potential failures.

Azure Resource Health

Azure Resource Health helps monitor the status of Azure resources and services. It provides insights into whether a particular resource, such as a Virtual Network Gateway or Load Balancer, is healthy or experiencing issues. Resource Health allows you to:

- **Track outages**: Monitor whether services are experiencing interruptions or degradation.

- **Access incident details**: View detailed information about resource health, including incidents, affected resources, and estimated recovery times.

This tool is essential for tracking the overall health of your network resources and identifying whether external factors, such as regional outages, are affecting your services.

Azure Service Health

While **Resource Health** provides insights into individual resource status, **Azure Service Health** offers a broader view of service-wide health and availability. It includes:

- **Service issues**: Provides notifications about issues with specific Azure services in the region.

- **Planned maintenance**: Alerts about upcoming maintenance that could affect the network.

- **Health advisories**: Notices about potential risks to services based on changes in Azure infrastructure.

Azure Service Health is particularly useful for understanding if external factors (e.g., Azure platform outages or planned maintenance) are impacting your network's performance.

Key Network Health Check Strategies

Now that we have explored the tools, let's discuss the best strategies for conducting network health checks in Azure. These practices will ensure that your network remains resilient, optimized, and secure.

1. Regular Connectivity Testing

Verifying the connectivity between various network components is the first step in any network health check. This includes:

- **VM-to-VM connectivity**: Check if VMs in the same VNet or across VNets can communicate with each other.
- **VNet-to-Internet connectivity**: Ensure that VMs or services requiring internet access are able to reach external websites or services.
- **End-to-End Communication**: For services such as web applications, ensure that the full path (client to application) is functioning correctly.

Azure's **Connection Troubleshoot** and **IP Flow Verify** tools can help you test these connectivity scenarios in real-time.

2. Monitor Network Security Configurations

Ensuring that your security configurations are intact is crucial for maintaining the integrity of your network. The following areas should be routinely checked:

- **NSG Rules**: Verify that NSGs are correctly configured to allow or deny traffic based on your security policies.
- **Application Gateway WAF Rules**: If using an Application Gateway with Web Application Firewall (WAF), ensure that your rules are up to date and not overly restrictive.

- **Azure Firewall Policies**: Regularly audit firewall policies to ensure that they are correctly allowing or blocking traffic as intended.

- **Route Tables**: Ensure that the route tables are configured to correctly direct traffic between VNets, on-premises networks, and the internet.

Use **NSG Flow Logs** and **Azure Firewall Logs** to gain insights into how traffic is being allowed or blocked across your network.

3. Network Performance Monitoring

Performance issues can often arise due to high traffic, misconfigured resources, or insufficient resource allocation. To avoid performance bottlenecks, the following should be monitored:

- **Throughput**: Monitor network throughput for individual resources (e.g., VNets, VPN Gateways, Load Balancers) to ensure that they are operating within expected performance thresholds.

- **Latency**: Measure the round-trip time (RTT) between network components to detect high-latency issues.

- **Traffic Patterns**: Analyze traffic flow to detect any unexpected traffic spikes or packet loss.

Use **Azure Monitor Metrics** and **Network Watcher Metrics** to track performance over time and create alerts for abnormal behavior.

4. Review Network Topology and Architecture

Over time, the network architecture may evolve, which can lead to configuration drift. A periodic review of your network's topology ensures that it still matches your intended design. Key areas to review include:

- **Virtual Network Peering**: Ensure that peering relationships between VNets are functioning as expected.
- **Subnet Allocation**: Verify that subnets have been allocated correctly and are not oversubscribed.
- **Load Balancer Configuration**: Ensure that load balancing rules are correctly distributing traffic across backend resources.
- **ExpressRoute and VPN Gateways**: Review the configuration and performance of ExpressRoute or VPN Gateway connections to ensure that hybrid connectivity is optimal.

Use **Azure Network Watcher Topology** to visualize and review the network topology.

5. Proactive Alerting

Setting up proactive alerts is essential for catching potential issues before they turn into critical failures. Alerts can be configured to notify administrators or trigger automated remediation scripts in response to:

- **Performance anomalies**: Such as unusually high or low throughput, high latency, or dropped packets.

- **Security violations**: For instance, when a rule in an NSG or firewall denies unexpected traffic.

- **Configuration issues**: Such as route misconfigurations or failed connections.

Use **Azure Monitor Alerts** to set up these automated notifications and integrate them with **Action Groups** to send messages through multiple channels like email, SMS, or webhooks.

6. Automating Network Health Checks

Automation can help you streamline regular health check tasks. For example, you can create scheduled tasks using **Azure Automation** to:

- Run network performance tests periodically.

- Check the status of critical network resources (e.g., VPN Gateways, Load Balancers).

- Review NSG flow logs and generate alerts when anomalous patterns are detected.

Automation can significantly reduce manual effort and ensure that network health checks are performed consistently and on time.

Conclusion

Network health checks are an essential aspect of managing a secure, high-performing, and resilient network in Azure. By leveraging tools like **Azure Network Watcher**, **Azure Monitor**, and **Azure Service Health**, along with following best practices for security, performance, and configuration integrity, you can ensure that your

Azure network infrastructure operates optimally. Regular health checks, proactive alerting, and automation can help you identify and address potential issues before they impact users or operations, keeping your network running smoothly and securely at all times.

Chapter 8: Automation and Infrastructure as Code

ARM Templates for Network Deployment

Azure Resource Manager (ARM) templates are JSON-based configuration files used to define and deploy Azure infrastructure in a repeatable and declarative manner. By using ARM templates, network architects and administrators can codify infrastructure definitions, streamline deployments, enforce configuration standards, and improve overall DevOps practices. In this section, we'll explore the structure of ARM templates, how to write them for networking resources, deployment strategies, parameterization, modularization, and best practices to ensure maintainability and scalability.

Why Use ARM Templates?

Manual deployment via the Azure Portal is suitable for learning or small environments, but it doesn't scale. ARM templates offer the following benefits:

- **Repeatability**: Deploy the same infrastructure across multiple environments (dev, test, prod).
- **Version Control**: Store templates in Git to track changes and manage collaboration.
- **Auditability**: Maintain an immutable history of infrastructure changes.
- **Automation**: Integrate with CI/CD pipelines for continuous infrastructure delivery.

- **Standardization**: Enforce naming, tagging, and security conventions at scale.

Using ARM templates is a cornerstone of infrastructure as code (IaC), enabling consistency across deployments and reducing human error.

Anatomy of an ARM Template

ARM templates are JSON documents structured into four main sections:

1. **$schema**: The location of the template schema file.
2. **contentVersion**: Version of the template (user-defined).
3. **parameters**: Inputs used to make the template dynamic.
4. **variables**: Reusable values derived from parameters or expressions.
5. **resources**: The Azure resources to be deployed.
6. **outputs**: Values returned after the template is deployed.

Here's a basic scaffold of an ARM template for a virtual network:

```
{

"$schema": "https://schema.management.azure.com/schemas/2019-04-01/deploymentTemplate.json#",

"contentVersion": "1.0.0.0",

"parameters": {

"vnetName": {

"type": "string",

"defaultValue": "myVNet"
```

```
},
"addressPrefix": {
"type": "string",
"defaultValue": "10.0.0.0/16"
}
},
"resources": [
{
"type": "Microsoft.Network/virtualNetworks",
"apiVersion": "2022-01-01",
"name": "[parameters('vnetName')]",
"location": "[resourceGroup().location]",
"properties": {
"addressSpace": {
"addressPrefixes": [
"[parameters('addressPrefix')]"
]
}
}
}
```

]

}

Deploying ARM Templates

ARM templates can be deployed through various tools:

- **Azure Portal** (via "Deploy a custom template")
- **Azure CLI**:

```
az deployment group create \
—resource-group MyResourceGroup \
—template-file vnet-template.json \
—parameters vnetName=myVNet addressPrefix=10.1.0.0/16
```

- **PowerShell**:

```
New-AzResourceGroupDeployment `
-ResourceGroupName "MyResourceGroup" `
-TemplateFile "vnet-template.json" `
-vnetName "myVNet" `
-addressPrefix "10.1.0.0/16"
```

- **ARM Template REST API**
- **Azure DevOps Pipelines** or **GitHub Actions**

Parameterization

To make templates reusable and environment-agnostic, use parameters for values like names, IP ranges, and tags. Parameters can have types (string, int, bool, array, object) and include default values, allowed values, and constraints.

```
"parameters": {

"environment": {

"type": "string",

"allowedValues": ["dev", "test", "prod"],

"defaultValue": "dev"

}

}
```

You can then use the value of environment in resource naming:

```
"name": "[concat(parameters('environment'), '-vnet')]"
```

Modular Templates and Linked Deployments

For complex environments, it's better to split templates into smaller, modular components. You can link templates together using Microsoft.Resources/deployments.

Example Structure:

- mainTemplate.json
- networking/vnet.json

- networking/nsg.json

In mainTemplate.json:

```
{
"resources": [
{
"type": "Microsoft.Resources/deployments",
"apiVersion": "2021-04-01",
"name": "vnetDeployment",
"properties": {
"mode": "Incremental",
"templateLink": {
"uri": "<URL-to-vnet.json>",
"contentVersion": "1.0.0.0"
},
"parameters": {
"vnetName": {
"value": "[parameters('vnetName')]"
}
}
}
```

```
}
]
}
```

This approach encourages reuse and makes debugging simpler.

Conditional Logic and Copy Loops

ARM templates support conditions and loops to simplify logic like:

- Only deploying a resource if a condition is met
- Deploying multiple subnets dynamically

Example: Conditional NSG Creation

```
"condition": "[equals(parameters('createNSG'), 'true')]"
```

Example: Subnet Loop

```
"copy": {
"name": "subnetLoop",
"count": "[length(parameters('subnets'))]"
}
```

Output Values

Use outputs to return useful information after deployment—e.g., resource IDs, IP addresses, or connection strings.

```
"outputs": {
```

```
"vnetId": {
"type": "string",
"value":              "[resourceId('Microsoft.Network/virtualNetworks',
parameters('vnetName'))]"
}
}
```

You can reference these in scripts or downstream pipelines.

Best Practices

1. **Use incremental deployments**: Avoid complete mode unless recreating the entire environment is intentional.
2. **Avoid hardcoding**: Always parameterize names, locations, and sensitive data.
3. **Validate templates** before deployment using:

```
az deployment group validate \
—resource-group MyResourceGroup \
—template-file template.json
```

1. **Use variables for reusability**: If a value is used multiple times, define it once as a variable.
2. **Document your templates**: Include metadata and comments in parameter files or version control.
3. **Leverage secure parameter files**: Avoid storing secrets in plain JSON; use Azure Key Vault where applicable.
4. **Format and lint**: Use tools like Visual Studio Code ARM Tools extension for formatting and validation.
5. **Source control**: Store templates in Git and use pull

request workflows to manage changes.

6. **Lock down deployments**: Use role-based access control (RBAC) and resource locks to prevent unauthorized or accidental changes.

Sample Real-World Scenario: Network Stack

In a production-ready template, you might deploy:

- Virtual Network with address space
- Multiple subnets
- NSGs per subnet
- Route tables with UDRs
- Peering configuration
- Diagnostic settings for logs

This template could be 500+ lines and modularized across files. You can orchestrate this as part of your CI/CD pipeline, ensuring every environment (from dev to prod) has a consistent network baseline.

Conclusion

ARM templates are a foundational tool for automating network deployment in Azure. By abstracting infrastructure into declarative JSON files, teams gain better control, consistency, and auditability over their cloud environments. Whether you're deploying simple VNets or complex multi-region architectures, ARM templates enable you to codify your designs and scale them reliably across your organization. Embracing ARM within your DevOps workflow ensures that your Azure networking is not only robust but also agile and secure.

Using Bicep for Declarative Configuration

Bicep is a domain-specific language (DSL) developed by Microsoft to simplify the authoring of Azure Resource Manager (ARM) templates. It provides a cleaner syntax, improved readability, better tooling support, and eliminates much of the complexity and verbosity associated with traditional ARM JSON templates. This makes Bicep an ideal choice for modern infrastructure as code (IaC) practices in Azure.

In this section, we will cover the architecture of Bicep, how to write Bicep templates specifically for networking resources, how to organize reusable modules, integrate Bicep into CI/CD pipelines, and follow best practices for managing Bicep files at scale.

Benefits of Bicep over ARM JSON

Bicep is not a replacement for the Azure Resource Manager; instead, it transpiles down to standard ARM JSON. However, it brings several advantages:

- **Simplified syntax**: Fewer lines of code and no brackets within brackets.
- **Intellisense support**: Rich autocomplete and type checking in Visual Studio Code.
- **Modularization**: Supports reusability with modules.
- **No need to write JSON**: Automatically compiles into ARM-compatible templates.

- **Better parameter management**: Strong typing and parameter validations built in.

A Bicep file is .bicep and is compiled to .json using the Bicep CLI.

Installing and Compiling Bicep

To start using Bicep, you can install it via the Azure CLI:

az bicep install

Once installed, you can compile a .bicep file to ARM JSON using:

az bicep build—file main.bicep

Or deploy it directly to Azure:

az deployment group create \

—resource-group MyResourceGroup \

—template-file main.bicep

Basic Structure of a Bicep File

A typical Bicep file includes:

- **Parameters**: Inputs such as resource names, IP ranges, or booleans.
- **Variables**: Computed values or reusable strings.
- **Resources**: The actual Azure resources to deploy.
- **Modules**: Reusable components called from other files.

- **Outputs**: Returned values such as resource IDs or IP addresses.

Example: Simple Virtual Network

```
param location string = resourceGroup().location

param vnetName string = 'myVnet'

param addressPrefix string = '10.0.0.0/16'

resource vnet 'Microsoft.Network/virtualNetworks@2022-05-01' = {

name: vnetName

location: location

properties: {

addressSpace: {

addressPrefixes: [

addressPrefix

]

}

}

}
```

This defines a basic virtual network with a single address prefix.

Defining Subnets and NSGs

Subnets can be embedded within the VNet or created as separate resources:

```
param subnetName string = 'default'

param subnetPrefix string = '10.0.0.0/24'

resource subnet 'Microsoft.Network/virtualNetworks/subnets@2022-05-01' = {

parent: vnet

name: subnetName

properties: {

addressPrefix: subnetPrefix

}

}
```

To associate a subnet with an NSG:

```
resource nsg 'Microsoft.Network/networkSecurityGroups@2022-05-01' = {

name: '${subnetName}-nsg'

location: location

properties: {

securityRules: [

{
```

```
name: 'AllowHTTP'
properties: {
priority: 100
direction: 'Inbound'
access: 'Allow'
protocol: 'Tcp'
sourcePortRange: '*'
destinationPortRange: '80'
sourceAddressPrefix: '*'
destinationAddressPrefix: '*'
}
}
]
}
}
resource subnetWithNSG 'Microsoft.Network/virtualNetworks/subnets@2022-05-01' = {
parent: vnet
name: subnetName
properties: {
addressPrefix: subnetPrefix
```

```
networkSecurityGroup: {
id: nsg.id
}
}
}
```

Using Modules for Reusability

Bicep modules allow you to break infrastructure into smaller, reusable units.

Example Directory Structure:

```
main.bicep
modules/
vnet.bicep
nsg.bicep
subnet.bicep
```

Example Module Usage in main.bicep:

```
module vnetModule './modules/vnet.bicep' = {
name: 'deployVnet'
params: {
vnetName: 'coreVNet'
```

```
addressPrefix: '10.1.0.0/16'
location: location
}
}
```

And vnet.bicep:

```
param vnetName string
param addressPrefix string
param location string
resource vnet 'Microsoft.Network/virtualNetworks@2022-05-01' = {
name: vnetName
location: location
properties: {
addressSpace: {
addressPrefixes: [
addressPrefix
]
}
}
}
output vnetId string = vnet.id
```

Modules can be nested and referenced with outputs for complex deployments.

Secure Parameter Handling

Use parameter files (.bicepparam) to separate deployment configuration from logic:

```
// main.bicep

param vnetName string

param addressPrefix string

// main.bicepparam

using 'main.bicep'

param vnetName = 'secureVNet'

param addressPrefix = '10.2.0.0/16'
```

This is useful for maintaining different environments (dev, test, prod) with consistent structure.

Integrating with CI/CD

Bicep files can be deployed as part of pipelines in GitHub Actions or Azure DevOps. Example GitHub Actions workflow:

```
name: Deploy Bicep

on:

push:

branches:
```

```
- main
jobs:
deploy:
runs-on: ubuntu-latest
steps:
- uses: actions/checkout@v2
- name: Azure Login
uses: azure/login@v1
with:
creds: ${{ secrets.AZURE_CREDENTIALS }}
- name: Deploy Bicep File
run: |
az deployment group create \
—resource-group MyRG \
—template-file main.bicep
```

This enables automated infrastructure delivery aligned with modern DevOps practices.

Advanced Features

Conditions

```
param deployNSG bool = true
```

```
resource nsg 'Microsoft.Network/networkSecurityGroups@2022-05-01' = if (deployNSG) {

name: 'myNSG'

location: location

properties: {}

}
```

Loops

```
param subnetNames array = ['subnet1', 'subnet2']

resource subnets 'Microsoft.Network/virtualNetworks/subnets@2022-05-01' = [for subnetName in subnetNames: {

name: subnetName

parent: vnet

properties: {

addressPrefix: '10.0.0.0/24'

}

}]
```

Resource Dependency

Bicep automatically handles dependencies based on references, but you can also use dependsOn explicitly when necessary.

Best Practices

- **Modularize**: Split infrastructure into logical components.
- **Use linting**: Run bicep build and bicep linter before commits.
- **Leverage outputs**: Pass data between modules and deployments.
- **Control versions**: Use version control and semantic naming.
- **Secure parameters**: Never hard-code secrets; use Key Vault.
- **Keep templates DRY**: Use parameters and variables extensively.
- **Test locally**: Use az deployment sub what-if to preview changes.

Conclusion

Bicep offers a powerful, streamlined, and maintainable way to define Azure infrastructure as code. Its declarative syntax, strong typing, modular support, and seamless integration with Azure tooling make it a future-proof solution for deploying complex network topologies and environments. By adopting Bicep, teams can improve development velocity, reduce manual errors, enforce policy compliance, and deliver reliable infrastructure at scale. Whether deploying VNets, subnets, NSGs, or route tables, Bicep brings simplicity and automation to the forefront of Azure networking.

Network Automation with PowerShell and Azure CLI

Automating Azure network deployments and management tasks with scripting tools is an essential practice for modern cloud operations. PowerShell and the Azure CLI (Command-Line Interface) are powerful tools that allow engineers to interact programmatically with Azure resources, reduce human error, enforce standardization, and boost productivity. This section provides an in-depth guide on using both PowerShell and Azure CLI for common and advanced Azure networking tasks, including deploying VNets, managing subnets and NSGs, peering VNets, configuring VPN gateways, and auditing configurations.

Why Automate Networking Tasks?

Manual processes are time-consuming, error-prone, and inconsistent. Automation via PowerShell and Azure CLI offers:

- **Repeatability** – Scripts can be reused across environments.
- **Speed** – Create and configure resources in seconds.
- **Scalability** – Manage thousands of resources through loops and logic.
- **Integration** – Easily incorporated into CI/CD pipelines and DevOps flows.
- **Governance** – Ensure compliance through scripted validation and reporting.

PowerShell is particularly suited to Windows-heavy environments and supports object-based operations. Azure CLI is cross-platform, easier for newcomers, and preferred for simple, fast operations.

Getting Started

Install Azure CLI

Azure CLI is available on Windows, macOS, and Linux.

az version

az upgrade

Install Azure PowerShell

Install the Az module:

Install-Module -Name Az -AllowClobber -Scope CurrentUser

Import-Module Az

Login:

Connect-AzAccount

Or in CLI:

az login

Creating a Virtual Network

Azure CLI

az network vnet create \

—resource-group MyRG \

—name MyVNet \

—address-prefix 10.0.0.0/16 \

—subnet-name WebSubnet \

—subnet-prefix 10.0.1.0/24

PowerShell

$subnet = New-AzVirtualNetworkSubnetConfig -Name "WebSubnet" -AddressPrefix "10.0.1.0/24"

$vnet = New-AzVirtualNetwork -ResourceGroupName "MyRG" -Location "EastUS" `

-Name "MyVNet" -AddressPrefix "10.0.0.0/16" -Subnet $subnet

You can add more subnets later using Add-AzVirtualNetworkSubnetConfig.

Managing Network Security Groups (NSGs)

NSGs control traffic to and from Azure resources.

Create and Configure with Azure CLI

az network nsg create—resource-group MyRG—name WebNSG

az network nsg rule create \

—resource-group MyRG \

—nsg-name WebNSG \

—name AllowHTTP \

—protocol Tcp \

—direction Inbound \

—priority 100 \

—source-address-prefix '*' \

—source-port-range '*' \

—destination-address-prefix '*' \

—destination-port-range 80 \

—access Allow

PowerShell

$nsgRule = New-AzNetworkSecurityRuleConfig -Name "AllowHTTP" `

-Protocol "Tcp" -Direction "Inbound" -Priority 100 `

-SourceAddressPrefix "*" -SourcePortRange "*" `

-DestinationAddressPrefix "*" -DestinationPortRange 80 `

-Access "Allow"

$nsg = New-AzNetworkSecurityGroup -ResourceGroupName "MyRG" `

-Location "EastUS" -Name "WebNSG" -SecurityRules $nsgRule

To associate an NSG with a subnet:

$vnet = Get-AzVirtualNetwork -Name "MyVNet" -ResourceGroupName "MyRG"

$subnet = Get-AzVirtualNetworkSubnetConfig -Name "WebSubnet" -VirtualNetwork $vnet

$subnet.NetworkSecurityGroup = $nsg

Set-AzVirtualNetwork -VirtualNetwork $vnet

VNet Peering Automation

VNet peering connects two VNets for seamless private communication.

CLI

az network vnet peering create \

—name Link1 \

—resource-group MyRG \

—vnet-name VNet1 \

—remote-vnet VNet2ID \

—allow-vnet-access

Use az network vnet show to retrieve the ID of the remote VNet.

PowerShell

$vnet1 = Get-AzVirtualNetwork -Name "VNet1" -ResourceGroupName "MyRG"

```
$vnet2 = Get-AzVirtualNetwork -Name "VNet2" -ResourceGroupName "MyRG"

Add-AzVirtualNetworkPeering -Name "Link1" `

-VirtualNetwork $vnet1 `

-RemoteVirtualNetworkId $vnet2.Id `

-AllowVirtualNetworkAccess
```

Repeat in reverse to establish bi-directional peering.

Deploying VPN Gateways

VPN gateways enable secure site-to-site or point-to-site connections.

Create Public IP for Gateway

```
az network public-ip create \

—resource-group MyRG \

—name VpnGatewayIP \

—sku Standard \

—allocation-method Static
```

Create Gateway Subnet

```
az network vnet subnet create \

—resource-group MyRG \

—vnet-name MyVNet \
```

—name GatewaySubnet \

—address-prefix 10.0.255.0/27

Create VPN Gateway

az network vnet-gateway create \

—name MyVpnGateway \

—resource-group MyRG \

—vnet MyVNet \

—public-ip-address VpnGatewayIP \

—gateway-type Vpn \

—vpn-type RouteBased \

—sku VpnGw1 \

—no-wait

Auditing and Compliance Scripts

List NSG Rules for All Subnets

az network nsg list—query "[].{Name:name, Location:location}" -o table

PowerShell to Find Open Ports

$nsgs = Get-AzNetworkSecurityGroup

foreach ($nsg in $nsgs) {

$nsg.SecurityRules | Where-Object { $_.Access -eq "Allow" -and $_.Direction -eq "Inbound" -and $_.DestinationPortRange -eq "3389" }

}

This helps identify open RDP ports across the subscription.

Scripting Multi-Region Network Deployments

You can script VNet and NSG creation in multiple regions dynamically.

CLI Example with Loops (using Bash)

for region in eastus westus; do

az network vnet create—name "VNet-$region"—resource-group MyRG \

—location $region—address-prefix 10.0.0.0/16 \

—subnet-name "Subnet1"—subnet-prefix 10.0.1.0/24

done

PowerShell Example with Loop

$regions = @("EastUS", "WestUS")

foreach ($region in $regions) {

New-AzVirtualNetwork -Name "VNet-$region" -ResourceGroupName "MyRG" `

-Location $region -AddressPrefix "10.0.0.0/16" `

-Subnet @(New-AzVirtualNetworkSubnetConfig -Name "Subnet1" -AddressPrefix "10.0.1.0/24")

}

Using Automation Accounts

For recurring tasks, use **Azure Automation Accounts** to schedule PowerShell or Python scripts that:

- Audit NSGs
- Rotate IP whitelists
- Run connection tests
- Export route tables to storage

CI/CD Integration

Include networking scripts in your Azure DevOps or GitHub pipelines.

Example Azure CLI task in Azure DevOps YAML:

- task: AzureCLI@2

inputs:

azureSubscription: 'MyServiceConnection'

scriptType: 'bash'

scriptLocation: 'inlineScript'

inlineScript: |

az network vnet create—resource-group $(rgName)—name $(vnetName)—address-prefix 10.1.0.0/16

This ensures infrastructure changes are reviewed, versioned, and repeatable.

Best Practices

- **Parameterize scripts**: Use variables and input arguments to avoid hardcoding.
- **Use tagging consistently**: Add—tags to CLI commands or -Tag in PowerShell to support resource governance.
- **Test scripts in dev environments** before running in production.
- **Include error handling and logging** in complex scripts.
- **Store scripts in version control** and peer review them through pull requests.
- **Use az deployment what-if or Test-AzDeployment** for safe previews of changes.

Conclusion

Automation with PowerShell and Azure CLI empowers teams to manage networking at scale with consistency, speed, and reliability. These tools provide deep integration with Azure APIs and support a wide range of use cases—from basic deployments to advanced configuration, auditing, and CI/CD integration. Mastering these scripting approaches equips cloud professionals to build robust, secure, and scalable networks that align with modern DevOps and infrastructure as code principles.

Integrating with DevOps Pipelines

Integrating Azure networking infrastructure into DevOps pipelines enables continuous delivery, standardized deployments, and compliance-driven governance. Whether you're building out a new virtual network, managing NSG rules, deploying VPN configurations, or updating DNS records, automating these tasks through CI/CD pipelines ensures consistency, traceability, and efficiency. This section explores how to integrate networking infrastructure deployments into popular DevOps pipelines using Azure DevOps and GitHub Actions, covering everything from file organization and pipeline setup to secrets management, testing, and environment promotion.

The Case for DevOps in Network Engineering

Traditional infrastructure provisioning is manual, error-prone, and slow. Networking, in particular, has lagged behind application development in terms of agility. By bringing networking into the DevOps pipeline, organizations gain:

- **Automated change control**
- **Environment parity (dev/stage/prod)**
- **Improved auditability**
- **Peer-reviewed infrastructure as code**
- **Rapid rollback in case of failure**

- **Zero-touch deployment for critical updates**

This approach aligns with GitOps principles: infrastructure defined as code, version-controlled, and automatically applied via CI/CD.

Prerequisites and Tools

Before implementing CI/CD for networking, ensure the following:

- Azure subscription and service principal for authentication
- Infrastructure code in Bicep, ARM, PowerShell, or CLI scripts
- Pipeline platform (Azure DevOps, GitHub Actions, etc.)
- Secret management (Key Vault, GitHub Secrets, DevOps Library)
- State management (optional, for tools like Terraform)

Organizing Your Repository

A typical repository structure for Azure networking might look like:

/infrastructure/

/modules/

vnet.bicep

nsg.bicep

dns.bicep

/envs/

dev.bicepparam

prod.bicepparam

main.bicep

pipeline/

deploy.yml

validate.yml

Keep environment-specific parameters separate to allow isolated deployments and simplify testing.

Using Azure DevOps Pipelines

Azure DevOps supports YAML-based pipelines for full control and flexibility.

Example: Deploying Bicep Templates

trigger:

branches:

include:

- main

variables:

azureSubscription: 'MyServiceConnection'

resourceGroup: 'MyRG'

```
templateFile: 'infrastructure/main.bicep'
parameterFile: 'infrastructure/envs/dev.bicepparam'
stages:
- stage: Validate
jobs:
- job: Validate
pool:
vmImage: 'ubuntu-latest'
steps:
- checkout: self
- task: AzureCLI@2
inputs:
azureSubscription: $(azureSubscription)
scriptType: 'bash'
scriptLocation: 'inlineScript'
inlineScript: |
az deployment group validate \
—resource-group $(resourceGroup) \
—template-file $(templateFile) \
—parameters @$(parameterFile)
```

```
- stage: Deploy
dependsOn: Validate
jobs:
- job: DeployNetwork
pool:
vmImage: 'ubuntu-latest'
steps:
- checkout: self
- task: AzureCLI@2
inputs:
azureSubscription: $(azureSubscription)
scriptType: 'bash'
scriptLocation: 'inlineScript'
inlineScript: |
az deployment group create \
—resource-group $(resourceGroup) \
—template-file $(templateFile) \
—parameters @$(parameterFile)
```

Using GitHub Actions

GitHub Actions provides seamless Git-based automation workflows.

Example: Networking Deployment Workflow

```
name: Deploy Azure Network
on:
push:
branches:
- main
jobs:
deploy:
runs-on: ubuntu-latest
steps:
- uses: actions/checkout@v3
- name: Azure Login
uses: azure/login@v1
with:
creds: ${{ secrets.AZURE_CREDENTIALS }}
- name: Deploy Network
run: |
az deployment group create \
—resource-group MyRG \
—template-file infrastructure/main.bicep \
```

—parameters @infrastructure/envs/dev.bicepparam

Secrets like AZURE_CREDENTIALS can be generated using a service principal and stored securely in GitHub.

Approval Gates and Environment Promotion

For production deployments, it's critical to implement gating mechanisms such as:

- **Pull Request Reviews**
- **Manual Approvals**
- **Branch Protections**
- **Environment Tags**
- **Release Pipelines with Gates**

In Azure DevOps:

- Use Environments and Approvals to protect production.
- Define variables scoped per environment for things like region, SKU, or NSG rules.
- Use deployment conditions such as:

condition: and(succeeded(), eq(variables['Build.SourceBranch'], 'refs/heads/main'))

Validating Templates Before Deployment

Always validate infrastructure changes before applying them:

With Azure CLI:

```
az deployment group what-if \
—resource-group MyRG \
—template-file main.bicep \
—parameters @prod.bicepparam
```

PowerShell Equivalent:

```
Test-AzDeployment -ResourceGroupName "MyRG" `
-TemplateFile "main.bicep" `
-TemplateParameterFile "prod.bicepparam"
```

In CI, add a validation job before deployment and configure it to block further stages if validation fails.

Rolling Back Failed Deployments

While Azure deployments are idempotent, failed updates can leave resources in inconsistent states. To manage rollbacks:

- **Use Git revert** to roll back to a previous infrastructure commit.
- **Deploy tagged releases** (e.g., v1.3.0) instead of unversioned latest.
- **Keep stateful resources in separate templates** to avoid unintended destruction.

- **Use mode: incremental** instead of complete to avoid deletions.

Change Auditing and Compliance

CI/CD pipelines offer built-in audit trails:

- Who changed what, when, and why (via Git history)
- Approval comments and timestamps
- Deployment logs and exit codes
- Notifications via Teams, Email, Slack

Leverage this to meet compliance standards like ISO 27001, SOC 2, or HIPAA.

Secrets and Sensitive Data

Never store secrets directly in templates or scripts. Instead:

- Use Azure Key Vault references in Bicep:

```
param vpnSharedKey string = '@Microsoft.KeyVault(SecretUri=https://myvault.vault.azure.net/secrets/sharedKey)'
```

- In Azure DevOps, link Key Vault to a variable group.
- In GitHub, use encrypted secrets and restrict write access to workflows.

Testing Infrastructure Code

Incorporate testing before and after deployment:

- **Linting** (e.g., bicep build, bicep linter)
- **Static Analysis** (e.g., PSRule for Bicep)
- **Security scanning** (e.g., Checkov, TFLint for Terraform equivalents)
- **Post-deployment integration tests** (e.g., ping, DNS, NSG validation)

Example test step in CI:

az network vnet show—name VNet1—resource-group MyRG

Best Practices

- **Treat infrastructure like application code**: Use branches, reviews, and versioning.
- **Fail early**: Add syntax validation and what-if analysis.
- **Use modular templates**: Break out NSG, VNet, and DNS into reusable Bicep files.
- **Automate environment promotion**: Dev → Test → Staging → Prod.
- **Use tagging**: Track resource ownership, environment, and cost center.
- **Centralize logs**: Output deployment logs to Azure Monitor or Log Analytics.

- **Use retries and idempotency**: Azure deployments may timeout or hit transient errors.

Conclusion

Integrating Azure network deployments into DevOps pipelines transforms the way teams manage cloud infrastructure. By leveraging tools like Azure DevOps and GitHub Actions, combined with infrastructure as code languages like Bicep, organizations can achieve repeatable, secure, and rapid deployments. Pipelines enforce standardization, reduce manual errors, and enable agile networking workflows that keep pace with evolving application demands. As cloud networks become increasingly complex, automation through CI/CD is no longer optional—it is essential for scalability, reliability, and compliance.

Chapter 9: Real-World Use Cases and Architectures

Secure Multi-Tenant SaaS Environments

Building a secure multi-tenant Software-as-a-Service (SaaS) environment in Azure requires thoughtful planning and implementation of networking strategies that isolate tenants while optimizing performance and resource usage. This section explores the architecture, security, and scalability considerations involved in creating a robust multi-tenant SaaS platform using Azure Virtual Networking components.

Understanding Multi-Tenancy in Azure

Multi-tenancy allows a single instance of an application to serve multiple customers (tenants), ensuring that each tenant's data is isolated and secure. In Azure, this model can be implemented in multiple ways depending on the desired level of isolation:

- **Shared Infrastructure**: All tenants share the same resources, but logical separation is enforced at the application and data level.
- **Isolated Infrastructure**: Each tenant has dedicated resources, including their own VNets, subnets, and even compute resources.
- **Hybrid Approach**: Combines shared compute resources with isolated networking or storage, offering a balance between cost and security.

The choice between these models impacts the virtual networking strategy. For secure multi-tenant applications, a hybrid or isolated model is often preferred.

Networking Architecture for Tenant Isolation

One of the most effective approaches for tenant isolation is the **hub-and-spoke** network topology. In this model:

- The **Hub VNet** contains shared services like application gateways, firewalls, logging, monitoring, and DevOps agents.

- Each **Spoke VNet** represents an individual tenant, with its own subnets, network security groups (NSGs), and optional firewalls.

- **VNet Peering** connects each spoke to the hub, enabling access to shared services while maintaining isolation between tenants.

Key Features

- **No Transitive Peering**: Traffic cannot automatically flow from one spoke to another through the hub, enforcing tenant isolation.

- **Route Tables and NSGs**: Control traffic between subnets and restrict access between tenants.

- **Azure Firewall/NSGs**: Centralized control to enforce policies, log access, and detect anomalies.

Deployment Steps Using Azure CLI

```
# Create the resource group

az group create—name SaaS-Network-RG—location eastus

# Create the hub VNet

az network vnet create \

—resource-group SaaS-Network-RG \

—name HubVNet \

—address-prefix 10.0.0.0/16 \

—subnet-name SharedServices \

—subnet-prefix 10.0.0.0/24

# Create a spoke VNet for TenantA

az network vnet create \

—resource-group SaaS-Network-RG \

—name TenantA-VNet \

—address-prefix 10.1.0.0/16 \

—subnet-name AppSubnet \

—subnet-prefix 10.1.0.0/24

# Peer spoke with hub

az network vnet peering create \

—name TenantA-to-Hub \
```

```
—resource-group SaaS-Network-RG \
—vnet-name TenantA-VNet \
—remote-vnet HubVNet \
—allow-vnet-access
az network vnet peering create \
—name Hub-to-TenantA \
—resource-group SaaS-Network-RG \
—vnet-name HubVNet \
—remote-vnet TenantA-VNet \
—allow-vnet-access
```

Secure Access Control

To restrict inter-tenant access:

- Use **custom route tables** that prevent traffic from flowing between spokes.
- Configure **NSGs** to limit traffic within the tenant VNet to necessary services only.
- Optionally deploy **Azure Firewall** in the hub to inspect traffic.

```
# Create an NSG for the tenant subnet
az network nsg create \
—resource-group SaaS-Network-RG \
```

```
—name TenantA-NSG
# Create a rule to allow only HTTPS traffic
az network nsg rule create \
—resource-group SaaS-Network-RG \
—nsg-name TenantA-NSG \
—name AllowHTTPS \
—priority 100 \
—direction Inbound \
—access Allow \
—protocol Tcp \
—destination-port-ranges 443 \
—source-address-prefixes Internet \
—destination-address-prefixes '*' \
—description "Allow HTTPS inbound traffic"
# Associate NSG with subnet
az network vnet subnet update \
—vnet-name TenantA-VNet \
—name AppSubnet \
—resource-group SaaS-Network-RG \
—network-security-group TenantA-NSG
```

DNS and Service Discovery

Each tenant may require DNS resolution for internal services. Options include:

- **Azure Private DNS Zones**: Provide private domain name resolution within VNets.

- **Custom DNS Forwarding**: Deploy DNS forwarders in the hub VNet to resolve names across VNets securely.

This setup allows tenants to resolve internal services without exposing DNS to the internet or other tenants.

Logging and Monitoring

Centralized logging is crucial in a multi-tenant setup. Use **Azure Monitor**, **Log Analytics**, and **Network Watcher**:

- Deploy **Network Watcher** in the hub region to monitor flow logs and diagnose connectivity.

- Use **Diagnostic Settings** to stream NSG, Firewall, and Application Gateway logs to a central **Log Analytics workspace**.

- Create alerts on suspicious traffic patterns or policy violations.

```
# Enable Network Watcher

az network watcher configure \

—resource-group SaaS-Network-RG \

—locations eastus \
```

```
—enabled true

# Set diagnostic settings for an NSG

az monitor diagnostic-settings create \

—name TenantA-NSG-Logs \

—resource $(az network nsg show—name TenantA-NSG—resource-group SaaS-Network-RG—query id -o tsv) \

—workspace /subscriptions/<sub-id>/resourceGroups/<log-rg>/providers/Microsoft.OperationalInsights/workspaces/<workspace-name> \

—logs '[{"category": "NetworkSecurityGroupEvent", "enabled": true}]'
```

Scaling the Architecture

As your SaaS platform grows:

- Use **Azure Policy** to enforce consistent configuration across tenant environments (e.g., mandatory use of NSGs).
- Automate tenant onboarding with **ARM templates** or **Bicep**.
- Use **Azure Lighthouse** if managing multiple tenants across subscriptions.

For high-scale scenarios:

- Consider **Virtual WAN** for managing large, geographically dispersed tenant networks.
- Use **Application Gateway with WAF** for multi-tenant traffic routing, with URL path-based rules and custom domain support.

Considerations for Tenant Billing and Resource Metering

Azure does not natively bill per tenant in a shared environment. To enable internal cost metering:

- Tag all tenant resources consistently (e.g., TenantID, Environment).
- Use **Azure Cost Management + Billing** with custom filters to generate usage reports per tenant.
- For infrastructure isolation, deploy tenant environments in separate subscriptions.

Security Best Practices

- Implement **Just-in-Time (JIT) VM access** to reduce attack surface.
- Regularly review NSG and Firewall rules.
- Conduct penetration testing and threat modeling for new tenant features.
- Use **Azure Security Center** to assess and remediate security misconfigurations.

Summary

Designing a secure multi-tenant SaaS environment in Azure involves careful planning of networking, access control, monitoring, and scalability. Leveraging Azure's native features such as hub-and-spoke topology, NSGs, VNet peering, and centralized logging, you can isolate tenant traffic, enforce governance, and maintain a high level of security. As tenant counts grow, automation and policy enforcement become essential to maintain consistency and compliance.

The next sections will explore how similar architectural principles apply to other domains, including scalable e-commerce and regulated sectors like healthcare and finance.

Scalable E-Commerce Network Design

E-commerce platforms are among the most demanding workloads in the cloud. They must support unpredictable traffic surges, maintain high availability and performance, and enforce strict security and compliance requirements. Azure Virtual Networking provides a robust foundation for designing scalable, secure, and performant e-commerce architectures that can evolve with the business.

This section outlines a comprehensive, production-grade network design for a scalable e-commerce platform using Azure services. It also explores key considerations such as redundancy, security, automation, and integration with third-party services.

Architectural Overview

A scalable e-commerce network typically includes:

- **Frontend Layer**: Web applications and APIs accessible over HTTPS.
- **Application Layer**: Business logic, shopping cart functionality, and authentication.
- **Data Layer**: SQL and NoSQL databases, caching services.
- **Shared Services Layer**: Logging, monitoring, CI/CD pipelines, DNS, key management.
- **Perimeter Security**: Azure Application Gateway with Web Application Firewall (WAF), Azure Firewall, DDoS Protection.

To accommodate growth and ensure performance, these components should be distributed across subnets and optionally across multiple regions.

Hub-and-Spoke Topology with Application Gateway

For large-scale deployments, a **hub-and-spoke** network topology ensures separation of concerns, ease of governance, and operational flexibility.

- **Hub VNet**: Contains Application Gateway (WAF-enabled), Azure Firewall, Bastion, and shared monitoring/logging services.
- **Spoke VNets**: Segregate the frontend, application, and data tiers.

This separation allows each layer to scale independently while keeping communication controlled and secure.

```
# Create a resource group

az group create—name Ecommerce-RG—location eastus

# Create the hub VNet

az network vnet create \

—name Ecommerce-HubVNet \

—resource-group Ecommerce-RG \

—location eastus \

—address-prefix 10.0.0.0/16 \

—subnet-name GatewaySubnet \

—subnet-prefix 10.0.0.0/24

# Create the frontend spoke

az network vnet create \

—name Frontend-SpokeVNet \

—resource-group Ecommerce-RG \

—address-prefix 10.1.0.0/16 \

—subnet-name WebAppSubnet \

—subnet-prefix 10.1.0.0/24
```

Each spoke is peered with the hub, and appropriate **route tables** and **NSGs** are configured to prevent lateral movement between spokes unless explicitly allowed.

Load Balancing and High Availability

At the edge of the network, Azure **Application Gateway** provides SSL termination, WAF protection, and load balancing.

- **WAF Policy**: Protects against common vulnerabilities like SQL injection, XSS, and bot attacks.
- **URL-based Routing**: Routes requests to the appropriate backend pool based on the path (e.g., /checkout, /cart, /api).
- **Autoscaling**: Automatically increases or decreases capacity based on traffic.

```
az network application-gateway create \

—name EcommerceAppGateway \

—location eastus \

—resource-group Ecommerce-RG \

—vnet-name Ecommerce-HubVNet \

—subnet GatewaySubnet \

—capacity 2 \

—sku WAF_v2 \

—http-settings-cookie-based-affinity Enabled \

—frontend-port 443
```

Behind the Application Gateway, Azure Load Balancer or **Azure Front Door** can be introduced to globally distribute traffic and enhance performance.

Network Security Best Practices

Securing an e-commerce network is essential. Best practices include:

- **NSGs** for subnet-level control of ingress/egress traffic.
- **Azure Firewall** for centralized threat detection and logging.
- **DDoS Protection Plan** to mitigate volumetric attacks.
- **Private Endpoints** for database and storage access.

Example NSG Configuration:

```
# Allow HTTPS traffic to frontend subnet

az network nsg rule create \

—resource-group Ecommerce-RG \

—nsg-name Frontend-NSG \

—name AllowHTTPS \

—priority 100 \

—direction Inbound \

—access Allow \

—protocol Tcp \

—destination-port-ranges 443 \
```

```
—source-address-prefixes Internet \

—destination-address-prefixes '*'
```

To limit exposure, ensure:

- Backend subnets deny internet access unless via NAT Gateway.
- Databases are only accessible from specific subnets.
- Admin access is restricted via **Just-in-Time VM Access** and **Azure Bastion**.

Identity and Access Management

Use **Managed Identities** for secure service-to-service authentication and eliminate hardcoded secrets.

- Deploy **Azure Key Vault** in the shared services subnet.
- Assign RBAC roles to VNets and services.
- Enforce **Conditional Access** and **Privileged Identity Management (PIM)** for administrators.

For example, an App Service accessing Key Vault:

```
# Assign Key Vault Reader role to the App Service

az role assignment create \

—assignee <app_service_principal_id> \

—role "Key Vault Reader" \
```

```
—scope /subscriptions/<sub-id>/resourceGroups/Ecommerce-RG/providers/Microsoft.KeyVault/vaults/<vault-name>
```

Caching and Performance Optimization

High traffic demands quick response times. Consider:

- **Azure Redis Cache** for session and cart data.
- **Azure Content Delivery Network (CDN)** to cache static assets at edge nodes.
- **Private Link** and **ExpressRoute** for private and fast data access.

Redis can be deployed in a dedicated subnet and accessed privately:

```
az redis create \
—name EcommerceRedis \
—resource-group Ecommerce-RG \
—location eastus \
—sku Premium \
—vm-size P1 \
—subnet-id <subnet-id>
```

Monitoring and Troubleshooting

Effective monitoring is vital in e-commerce to detect issues before they impact users. Use:

- **Azure Monitor** and **Application Insights** to track performance and exceptions.
- **Network Watcher** for packet capture and connection monitoring.
- **Log Analytics** for aggregating diagnostic logs from WAF, Firewall, and NSGs.

Set up alerts for:

- Unusual spikes in latency.
- Application errors beyond a threshold.
- Unauthorized access attempts.

```
az monitor metrics alert create \
—name HighLatencyAlert \
—resource-group Ecommerce-RG \
—scopes /subscriptions/<sub-id>/resourceGroups/Ecommerce-RG/providers/Microsoft.Insights/components/<app-insights-name> \
—condition "avg requests/duration > 5000" \
—description "Alert when average response time exceeds 5 seconds"
```

Scalability Considerations

To prepare for traffic surges (e.g., Black Friday):

- **Enable autoscale** on web and app services.

- Use **scale sets** for VMs hosting backend services.
- Implement **SQL elastic pools** or **Cosmos DB** for dynamic storage scalability.
- Deploy **Multi-Region Architecture** using Azure Traffic Manager or Front Door.

Each region would have its own set of VNets (cloned design), with traffic distributed based on geography or performance.

Infrastructure as Code

Use **Bicep** or **Terraform** to define and deploy your network architecture. For example, a Bicep module for a frontend VNet:

```
param location string

param vnetName string = 'frontend-vnet'

param subnetPrefix string = '10.1.0.0/24'

resource vnet 'Microsoft.Network/virtualNetworks@2021-02-01' = {

name: vnetName

location: location

properties: {

addressSpace: {

addressPrefixes: [

'10.1.0.0/16'

]
```

```
}
subnets: [
{
name: 'WebAppSubnet'
properties: {
addressPrefix: subnetPrefix
}
}
]
}
}
```

Integrate these deployments into **Azure DevOps** or **GitHub Actions** for CI/CD pipelines to streamline updates and ensure consistency.

Compliance and Governance

To meet PCI-DSS, GDPR, or ISO requirements:

- Enable **Azure Policy** to enforce configuration rules (e.g., encryption at rest, no public IPs).
- Use **Azure Blueprints** to apply compliant environments at scale.
- Audit network changes via **Activity Logs** and **Azure Defender**.

Tag resources with Environment, CostCenter, Owner, and Application for tracking and cost management.

az tag create—resource-id <resource-id>—tags Environment=Production Owner=EcommerceTeam

Summary

Designing a scalable e-commerce network in Azure involves balancing performance, security, flexibility, and operational efficiency. By leveraging hub-and-spoke topology, Application Gateway with WAF, Azure Firewall, and private connectivity options, e-commerce businesses can ensure their platforms remain secure, available, and performant under varying load conditions.

Automation and monitoring are crucial for maintaining service quality and responding to incidents quickly. With a well-architected network and disciplined DevOps practices, organizations can confidently scale their operations and provide a secure, reliable shopping experience for their customers.

Healthcare and Finance Sector Networking

The healthcare and finance sectors have stringent requirements for network security, data privacy, availability, and regulatory compliance. Deploying infrastructure in Azure for these industries requires precise configuration and best practices to ensure sensitive data is protected, access is controlled, and workloads are resilient. In this section, we will explore how to design Azure virtual networks to meet the complex demands of healthcare and finance organizations.

Industry-Specific Challenges

Healthcare

- **HIPAA Compliance**: Requires strong encryption, access control, and audit logging.
- **Protected Health Information (PHI)** must be isolated and securely processed.
- **Integration with on-premises systems** (e.g., EHRs, PACS) is common.
- Real-time workloads like **telemedicine and medical imaging** require low latency.

Finance

- **PCI DSS Compliance**: Requires segmentation of the cardholder data environment (CDE), strict access control, and monitoring.
- **Highly sensitive data** such as transactions and account information must be isolated and encrypted.
- **Real-time processing and fraud detection** demand high availability and low-latency connectivity.
- **Auditability and traceability** are mandatory for all network activities.

Azure provides the building blocks needed to meet these needs, including Virtual Networks (VNets), Private Endpoints, Azure

Firewall, Application Gateway, Network Security Groups (NSGs), and DDoS Protection.

Reference Architecture

A common architecture pattern for healthcare and finance is based on **multi-tier segmentation**, combined with **hub-and-spoke topology**, **private connectivity**, and **defense in depth** strategies.

Tiers include:

1. **Public Edge** (optional): Azure Front Door or Application Gateway with WAF.
2. **DMZ (Demilitarized Zone)**: Receives traffic from public edge, filters and routes internally.
3. **Application Tier**: Hosts APIs, services, and internal logic.
4. **Data Tier**: SQL, Cosmos DB, or third-party databases with private endpoints.
5. **Integration Tier**: Connects with on-premises systems via VPN or ExpressRoute.

Building the Network Topology

```
# Create core VNets

az network vnet create \

—name HubVNet \

—resource-group RegulatedInfraRG \

—address-prefix 10.0.0.0/16 \

—subnet-name FirewallSubnet \

—subnet-prefix 10.0.0.0/24
```

```
az network vnet create \
—name AppVNet \
—resource-group RegulatedInfraRG \
—address-prefix 10.1.0.0/16 \
—subnet-name AppSubnet \
—subnet-prefix 10.1.0.0/24
```

Each tier should reside in its own subnet, with **NSGs** controlling traffic flow and **route tables** enforcing next-hop rules. This enables full control of East-West and North-South traffic.

Enforcing Isolation and Access Controls

Healthcare and finance applications often require **air gaps** between environments (e.g., Dev, Test, Prod) and strict segmentation within production environments.

Key isolation strategies:

- Use **Private Link** for data access (SQL, Blob, Cosmos DB).
- **Disable public IPs** for VMs and databases.
- Use **Service Endpoints** or **Private Endpoints** to keep traffic on Microsoft's backbone.
- Apply **NSG rules** at subnet level with granular ports and IP ranges.

Example NSG rule for healthcare API tier:

```
az network nsg rule create \
—resource-group RegulatedInfraRG \
—nsg-name API-NSG \
—name AllowAppGateway \
—priority 100 \
—direction Inbound \
—access Allow \
—protocol Tcp \
—source-address-prefixes 10.0.1.0/24 \
—destination-port-ranges 443 \
—destination-address-prefixes '*' \
—description "Allow traffic from Application Gateway subnet"
```

Additionally, leverage **Azure Policy** to enforce compliance:

```
az policy assignment create \
—name EnforcePrivateLink \
—scope /subscriptions/<sub-id> \
—policy <private-link-policy-id>
```

VPN and ExpressRoute for Hybrid Integration

Healthcare and finance organizations often maintain on-premises systems that must integrate with Azure.

- **VPN Gateway**: Best for quick setup or dev/test environments.
- **ExpressRoute**: Recommended for production workloads that require low-latency, private, and resilient connectivity.

Use **VPN with BGP** to dynamically learn routes and enforce failover.

```
az network vpn-gateway create \

—name HealthcareVPNGateway \

—resource-group RegulatedInfraRG \

—vnet HubVNet \

—public-ip-address HealthcareVPNPublicIP \

—gateway-type Vpn \

—vpn-type RouteBased \

—sku VpnGw2 \

—asn 65515
```

For finance, consider **ExpressRoute with Microsoft peering** to access services like Azure Storage and SQL without going over the internet.

Encryption and Key Management

Compliance mandates all sensitive data must be encrypted at rest and in transit.

- Use **TLS 1.2+** across all endpoints.
- Enable **Azure Disk Encryption** and **SQL Transparent Data Encryption (TDE)**.
- Integrate with **Azure Key Vault** for key management.
- Enable **Customer-Managed Keys (CMK)** where required.

Key Vault should be in a secure, isolated subnet and accessed only by authorized services using **Managed Identities**.

```
az keyvault create \
—name FinanceKeyVault \
—resource-group RegulatedInfraRG \
—location eastus \
—enable-soft-delete true \
—enable-purge-protection true
```

Application Gateway with WAF

For secure frontend access, use **Application Gateway v2 with WAF**. Configure **OWASP rules** to protect against common attacks. Use **SSL termination**, **custom domain certificates**, and **rewrite rules** for compliance headers (e.g., HIPAA audit logging or PCI tracking).

Configure **path-based routing** to separate apps (e.g., billing, portal, reports) and enforce rate-limiting for brute-force prevention.

```
az network application-gateway waf-policy create \
```

```
—resource-group RegulatedInfraRG \
—name FinanceWAFPolicy \
—policy-settings '{"state":"Enabled","mode":"Prevention"}'
```

Monitoring, Auditing, and Alerting

Robust monitoring is critical for security and operational assurance.

Required Tools:

- **Azure Monitor**: Collect metrics and logs from all services.
- **Azure Sentinel**: SIEM solution for threat detection, alert correlation, and incident management.
- **Log Analytics**: Analyze NSG flows, firewall logs, and system events.
- **Network Watcher**: Diagnose and visualize traffic patterns.

Enable **Diagnostic Settings** for every NSG, Gateway, and App Gateway.

```
az monitor diagnostic-settings create \
—name NsgFlowLogs \
—resource <nsg-id> \
—workspace <log-analytics-workspace-id> \
```

—logs '[{"category": "NetworkSecurityGroupFlowEvent", "enabled": true}]'

Alerts and Automation

Create alerts for:

- Unauthorized access attempts.
- Data exfiltration activities.
- DDoS attacks.
- Policy violations.

Use **Logic Apps** or **Automation Runbooks** to auto-remediate incidents (e.g., isolate compromised VM).

Zero Trust Implementation

Zero Trust is essential in healthcare and finance, especially with remote work and third-party access. Core principles include:

- **Verify explicitly**: Always authenticate and authorize.
- **Least privilege access**: Grant minimum necessary permissions.
- **Assume breach**: Segment and monitor everything.

Azure services that support Zero Trust:

- **Azure AD Conditional Access**
- **Just-in-Time (JIT) VM Access**

- **Azure Bastion** for secure VM access
- **Private Link and NSGs** for segmentation

Business Continuity and Disaster Recovery (BCDR)

Business continuity is non-negotiable for these industries.

- Use **Availability Zones** for high availability.
- Geo-replicate storage and databases with **Geo-Redundant Storage (GRS)** and **Auto-failover groups** for SQL.
- Implement **Azure Site Recovery (ASR)** to replicate VMs to a secondary region.
- Regularly test **disaster recovery (DR) drills** and failover automation.

Compliance Management

Azure provides tools for tracking and enforcing compliance:

- **Microsoft Compliance Manager**: View compliance scores and manage assessments (e.g., HIPAA, PCI-DSS).
- **Azure Policy + Blueprints**: Apply compliant configurations and auditing at scale.
- **Activity Logs**: Track who did what, when, and where.

```
az policy assignment list—query "[?policyDefinitionId=='/providers/Microsoft.Authorization/policyDefinitions/audit-vm-managed-disk-encryption']"
```

Use tagging for classification:

```
az resource tag \
—tags Environment=Prod Sector=Healthcare Compliance=HIPAA \
—ids <resource-id>
```

Summary

Networking in healthcare and finance within Azure demands a meticulous approach to security, compliance, isolation, and monitoring. With the right design—based on tiered architecture, private connectivity, NSGs, WAFs, encryption, and continuous auditing—organizations can confidently run regulated workloads while satisfying both technical and legal requirements.

Azure provides the flexibility to scale and adapt these designs over time while maintaining a strong security posture, ensuring sensitive data is safe, and critical services remain available to users and patients alike.

Case Studies from Industry

The theoretical principles of Azure virtual networking come to life through real-world implementations. In this section, we explore detailed case studies from organizations across various sectors—including retail, logistics, education, and media—to illustrate how Azure's networking capabilities are applied at scale. These case studies highlight challenges, solutions, architectural decisions, and operational outcomes. They demonstrate how different Azure networking services can be combined to solve complex problems, ensure resilience, improve security, and optimize performance.

Case Study 1: Global Retailer – Modernizing Legacy Infrastructure

Business Need

A multinational retail chain with over 3,000 stores worldwide needed to modernize its data center infrastructure and move to the cloud. The primary goals were:

- **Reduce operational costs**
- **Enhance scalability for seasonal demand spikes**
- **Improve latency for customers using the online store globally**
- **Secure customer data to meet GDPR and CCPA regulations**

Network Architecture

- **Hub-and-spoke topology**
- **ExpressRoute for hybrid connectivity**
- **Azure Front Door for global traffic optimization**
- **Application Gateway with WAF for regional frontend security**
- **Private Link for secure data access to storage and SQL services**

- **Azure Firewall and NSGs for East-West and North-South traffic control**

Key Implementation

To support global operations and customer traffic, the retailer deployed Azure Front Door to route users to the nearest regional deployment.

```
az network front-door create \
—name RetailGlobalFrontDoor \
—resource-group RetailNetRG \
—backend-address RetailAppEastUS.contoso.com \
—accepted-protocols Https \
—frontend-endpoints RetailCustomerPortal
```

The retailer also implemented **Azure Application Gateway with autoscaling and WAF**, protecting regional APIs and web apps from OWASP Top 10 threats.

Sensitive services like inventory databases were accessible only through **Private Endpoints**, preventing data exfiltration over the internet.

Outcomes

- 38% reduction in latency for EU-based customers
- Improved compliance visibility through Azure Policy and Microsoft Defender for Cloud

- Infrastructure costs reduced by 27% within the first year
- 99.99% uptime maintained during Black Friday surge

Case Study 2: Logistics Company – Real-Time Vehicle Telemetry

Business Need

A logistics and fleet management company wanted to build a platform to:

- Collect and analyze real-time telemetry data from over 50,000 vehicles
- Integrate with external partners via APIs
- Ensure data security and regulatory compliance across regions
- Support thousands of concurrent device connections

Network Strategy

The solution included:

- **Azure IoT Hub** in isolated subnets
- **Azure Virtual WAN** to simplify branch-to-Azure connectivity
- **Azure Private DNS Zones** for secure service resolution

- **Custom NSG rules** to restrict traffic to telemetry ingestion pipelines

- **Central logging and threat detection** using Azure Monitor and Sentinel

Key Configuration

The company used **Virtual WAN with Secure Hub** to simplify connection of branch offices, warehouses, and IoT gateways to Azure.

```
az network virtual-wan create \
—name FleetGlobalWAN \
—resource-group FleetInfraRG \
—location westus2
az network vhub create \
—name FleetHub \
—resource-group FleetInfraRG \
—virtual-wan FleetGlobalWAN \
—address-prefix 10.100.0.0/16
```

Each vehicle streamed data to an **IoT Hub** in a dedicated subnet, with **custom routes** ensuring telemetry packets were routed to secure backend APIs.

Results

- Achieved real-time ingestion of 15,000 messages/sec with minimal latency
- Enabled secure B2B API access using Azure API Management with IP filtering
- Centralized policy enforcement across WAN regions
- Uptime of 99.98% over a 12-month period
- Reduced physical data center footprint by 50%

Case Study 3: Online Education Platform – Scaling During Global Surge

Context

A digital education provider with millions of users faced explosive growth during the pandemic. They needed to:

- Scale quickly without degrading user experience
- Secure sensitive student and assessment data
- Enable seamless content delivery across geographies
- Maintain GDPR and FERPA compliance

Network Design

- **Azure CDN** for fast content delivery

- **Application Gateway for WAF-protected frontend access**
- **Regional VNets for content generation and learning analytics services**
- **Azure Bastion and Just-in-Time VM Access** for administrative controls
- **Private Endpoints for data storage and database access**

Implementation Highlights

Using Azure CDN and Front Door allowed low-latency access to learning content globally. Internal microservices were split into VNets by domain (e.g., exams, courses, analytics) and connected via **VNet peering** with custom **route tables** and NSGs.

To protect sensitive content, all APIs were routed through WAF policies:

```
az network application-gateway waf-policy custom-rule create \

—policy-name EducationWAFPolicy \

—resource-group EduNetRG \

—rule-name BlockUnusualHeaders \

—priority 100 \

—rule-type MatchRule \

—match-conditions match-variables=RequestHeaders \
```

—operator Equals \

—values suspicious-header

Outcomes

- Handled a 600% traffic increase with zero downtime
- Maintained regional compliance via data localization and encryption
- Cut page load time by 43% globally
- Secured APIs with zero successful exploits or downtime events

---

Case Study 4: Media Streaming Service – Low Latency, High Bandwidth Network

Requirement

A video-on-demand platform needed to support:

- Global delivery of HD/4K content
- Scalable backend for content ingestion, transcoding, and analytics
- DDoS protection and WAF against bot scraping and credential stuffing attacks
- Secure, private ingestion from content creators

Network Blueprint

- **Azure Front Door Standard/Premium** for edge caching and SSL offloading
- **ExpressRoute for studio ingest traffic**
- **Dedicated media ingestion subnets**
- **Private Link for media asset storage and Cosmos DB access**
- **Firewall with threat intelligence-based filtering**

Practical Implementation

Studios used ExpressRoute for uploading raw footage to a private subnet where transcoding pipelines operated securely.

Azure Front Door offered intelligent routing and geo-redundancy. Application Gateway filtered access to APIs and dashboards.

Azure Policy ensured all resources used only private endpoints and encrypted traffic.

```
az policy assignment create \
—name MediaPrivateOnly \
—scope /subscriptions/<sub-id>/resourceGroups/MediaNetRG \
—policy "/providers/Microsoft.Authorization/policyDefinitions/enforce-private-link" \
—params '{"effect":{"value":"Deny"}}'
```

Achievements

- 72% reduction in streaming latency across APAC and EMEA
- 100% private asset ingestion pipeline
- API performance improved by 45% using Application Gateway autoscaling
- Achieved SOC 2 Type II compliance within 90 days

Cross-Industry Lessons

Across these industries, several key networking patterns emerge:

- **Hub-and-Spoke** and **Virtual WAN** topologies are foundational for scalable, secure design
- **Private Link**, **NSGs**, and **Azure Firewall** enforce secure access and segmentation
- **Application Gateway + WAF** is a go-to for secure app exposure
- **Monitoring via Azure Monitor, Sentinel, and Watcher** is crucial for operational insight
- **Compliance automation** using Azure Policy and tagging helps maintain governance

Azure Virtual Networking, when paired with the right architectural principles and security posture, supports a broad spectrum of industries with diverse requirements. These case studies demonstrate that with thoughtful planning and modern tooling, Azure can meet and exceed enterprise expectations, even under pressure or regulatory scrutiny.

Chapter 10: Appendices

Glossary of Terms

Understanding Azure Virtual Networking requires familiarity with a wide range of technical terms and acronyms. This glossary provides clear, concise definitions of essential concepts, protocols, and services mentioned throughout the book. Whether you're a beginner needing foundational knowledge or an experienced professional looking for quick reference, this glossary is designed to help clarify terminology critical to working effectively with Azure networking.

Azure Virtual Network (VNet)

A logically isolated network in Azure, allowing users to securely connect Azure resources, on-premises networks, and the internet.

Address Space

The IP address range assigned to a VNet. It is defined in CIDR (Classless Inter-Domain Routing) notation, such as 10.0.0.0/16.

Subnet

A sub-division of a VNet's address space used to group resources and apply network policies like NSGs and route tables.

CIDR (Classless Inter-Domain Routing)

Notation for describing IP address ranges. Example: 192.168.1.0/24 represents 256 addresses from 192.168.1.0 to 192.168.1.255.

VNet Peering

A mechanism that connects two VNets, enabling resources to communicate with each other using private IPs. Peering can be regional or global.

ExpressRoute

A dedicated private connection between an on-premises infrastructure and Azure, bypassing the public internet. It offers greater reliability and lower latency.

Site-to-Site VPN

A secure connection between an on-premises site and an Azure VNet using IPsec/IKE protocols over the internet.

Point-to-Site VPN

A VPN connection configured on individual devices to connect to an Azure VNet, often used for remote access.

IPsec (Internet Protocol Security)

A suite of protocols used to secure IP communications by authenticating and encrypting each IP packet.

IKE (Internet Key Exchange)

A protocol used to set up a secure, authenticated communications channel in IPsec.

Network Security Group (NSG)

A set of rules that allow or deny inbound or outbound traffic to network interfaces, VMs, and subnets.

Application Security Group (ASG)

Logical groupings of virtual machine NICs that simplify NSG rule management by enabling rule assignment based on application.

Route Table

Contains a set of rules (routes) used to determine where network traffic is directed. Often used to implement User-Defined Routes (UDRs).

User-Defined Routes (UDRs)

Custom routing rules in Azure that override system routes, enabling control over traffic flow in and out of subnets.

Azure Firewall

A managed, cloud-based network security service that protects Azure Virtual Network resources.

Azure DDoS Protection

Protects applications from Distributed Denial of Service (DDoS) attacks. Standard tier includes adaptive tuning and telemetry.

Azure Application Gateway

A layer 7 (application layer) load balancer that includes features such as SSL termination, cookie-based session affinity, and Web Application Firewall (WAF).

Web Application Firewall (WAF)

A feature of Application Gateway that protects web apps from common exploits and vulnerabilities based on OWASP rules.

Load Balancer

Distributes incoming network traffic across multiple resources to ensure availability and reliability. Azure provides both Basic and Standard SKUs.

Azure Bastion

A fully managed service that provides secure and seamless RDP/SSH access to VMs without exposing them to public IP addresses.

Virtual WAN

A networking service that provides optimized and automated branch-to-branch connectivity through Azure.

Hub-and-Spoke Topology

A network design where a central hub VNet connects to multiple spoke VNets, often used to isolate workloads or environments.

Private Endpoint

A network interface that connects privately and securely to a service powered by Azure Private Link.

Private Link

Enables private connectivity to Azure services via a private endpoint in your VNet.

Service Endpoint

Extends your VNet's private address space to Azure services over the Azure backbone network.

Network Watcher

A suite of tools for monitoring and diagnosing network issues, including packet capture, connection troubleshooting, and NSG flow logs.

Diagnostics Settings

Configuration that enables the export of logs and metrics to destinations like Log Analytics, Event Hubs, or a Storage Account.

Log Analytics

A tool within Azure Monitor that provides powerful query and visualization capabilities for log data collected from various sources.

Azure Monitor

A platform for collecting, analyzing, and acting on telemetry from Azure and on-premises environments.

Azure Policy

A governance tool that enables administrators to define and enforce policies that ensure resources are compliant with organizational standards.

Azure Blueprints

A service that helps deploy a repeatable set of Azure resources that adhere to organizational standards, including role assignments, policies, and ARM templates.

ARM (Azure Resource Manager)

The deployment and management service for Azure. Resources are managed using ARM templates, REST APIs, and Azure Portal.

Bicep

A domain-specific language (DSL) for deploying Azure resources declaratively. It is a more concise and readable alternative to ARM templates.

Infrastructure as Code (IaC)

The practice of managing infrastructure through code rather than manual processes, enabling repeatability and version control.

Azure DevOps

A suite of tools for development, testing, and deployment. Includes features like pipelines, repositories, and artifacts.

Azure CLI

A command-line tool to create and manage Azure resources.

PowerShell for Azure

A set of modules that enables automation and management of Azure resources using PowerShell.

DNS (Domain Name System)

A system that translates domain names to IP addresses. Azure provides DNS services for both public and private zones.

Private DNS Zone

A DNS zone that allows the use of custom domain names within a VNet without exposing them to the internet.

Availability Zone

Physically separate zones within an Azure region that offer high availability and fault tolerance.

Region Pairing

Azure automatically pairs regions to provide replication, disaster recovery, and data residency solutions.

Resource Group

A container that holds related Azure resources. Resource groups make it easier to manage and deploy resources as a unit.

Tagging

A method for labeling resources with metadata, such as environment, cost center, or owner, for management and billing.

NSG Flow Logs

Logs generated by Network Watcher that capture information about ingress and egress IP traffic through an NSG.

Threat Intelligence

A capability of Azure Firewall to allow or deny traffic based on real-time threat intelligence feeds.

SIEM (Security Information and Event Management)

Azure Sentinel is Microsoft's cloud-native SIEM that collects and analyzes security data from across the enterprise.

Just-in-Time VM Access

A security feature that reduces exposure by allowing access to virtual machines only when needed and for a limited time.

Azure Sentinel

A scalable, cloud-native SIEM and SOAR (Security Orchestration Automated Response) solution for intelligent security analytics.

Compliance Manager

A tool that helps manage compliance with regulations and standards, providing scorecards and actionable recommendations.

This glossary is not exhaustive but serves as a critical reference to reinforce your understanding as you work through Azure networking projects. For more advanced terminology and up-to-date definitions, refer to official Microsoft Azure documentation.

Resources for Further Learning

Mastering Azure Virtual Networking requires more than just theoretical knowledge—it requires continuous practice, real-world implementation, and a willingness to explore evolving features. In this section, we provide a curated collection of resources to support your ongoing learning journey. These resources span official documentation, hands-on labs, certifications, blogs, videos, community forums, and third-party tools. Whether you're preparing for certification, building enterprise-grade architectures, or troubleshooting complex deployments, the following learning avenues will prove invaluable.

Official Microsoft Resources

Microsoft Learn

Microsoft Learn is a free, interactive learning platform that provides step-by-step tutorials and assessments. It's ideal for both beginners and experienced professionals.

Recommended learning paths:

- *Secure and connect networks in Azure*

  https://learn.microsoft.com/en-us/training/paths/secure-connect-networks-azure/

- *Design and implement virtual networking in Azure*

  https://learn.microsoft.com/en-us/training/modules/intro-to-azure-virtual-network/

Each module includes interactive labs using the Microsoft Learn sandbox, quizzes to assess your knowledge, and downloadable resources for offline study.

Microsoft Docs

The **Azure Virtual Network documentation** is the definitive technical reference for every feature, service, and integration option:

- https://learn.microsoft.com/en-us/azure/virtual-network/

Some key articles:

- *Virtual network peering*

https://learn.microsoft.com/en-us/azure/virtual-network/virtual-network-peering-overview

- *Azure Firewall best practices*

https://learn.microsoft.com/en-us/azure/firewall/firewall-best-practices

- *Configure user-defined routes*

https://learn.microsoft.com/en-us/azure/virtual-network/tutorial-create-route-table-portal

Each article contains architecture diagrams, best practice recommendations, configuration examples, and links to supporting content.

Azure Architecture Center

The **Azure Architecture Center** provides high-level guidance, reference architectures, and solution playbooks. It is especially helpful when designing scalable, secure solutions:

- https://learn.microsoft.com/en-us/azure/architecture/

Top reference architectures:

- *Hub-spoke network topology*
- *Global web application with Azure Front Door*
- *Hybrid network with VPN and ExpressRoute*

Certification and Training Programs

Microsoft Certifications

Certifications not only validate your expertise but also guide structured learning. Relevant certifications include:

- **AZ-104: Microsoft Azure Administrator**

  Covers networking, identity, storage, and VM administration.

- **AZ-700: Designing and Implementing Microsoft Azure Networking Solutions**

  Focuses exclusively on networking, including routing, security, hybrid connectivity, and monitoring.

- **AZ-305: Designing Microsoft Azure Infrastructure Solutions**

  Teaches architecture principles for enterprise-grade systems including virtual networking.

Each certification has an associated learning path on Microsoft Learn with practice questions and lab simulations.

Third-Party Training Platforms

- **Pluralsight**: Offers in-depth courses on Azure networking, often taught by MVPs.https://www.pluralsight.com[4]

4. https://www.pluralsight.com/

- **A Cloud Guru / Linux Academy**: Known for hands-on, scenario-based learning with cloud sandboxes.
- **Udemy**: Budget-friendly options with community ratings. Look for instructors with Azure certifications.
- **Coursera / edX**: Feature courses created in partnership with Microsoft and top universities.

Hands-On Labs and Sandboxes

Azure Sandbox

Through Microsoft Learn, users gain free access to a temporary Azure environment to complete exercises without requiring a paid subscription.

- No credit card required
- Pre-provisioned for lab activities
- 1–4 hours of usage per module

GitHub Learning Labs

Microsoft provides a collection of infrastructure-as-code samples, templates, and complete solution designs via GitHub:

- https://github.com/Azure/azure-quickstart-templates
- https://github.com/Azure/Enterprise-Scale

You can clone, fork, and deploy these examples directly using the Azure CLI or Bicep.

Example: Deploying a VNet and NSG with Bicep

```
param location string = resourceGroup().location

resource vnet 'Microsoft.Network/virtualNetworks@2022-01-01' = {

name: 'my-vnet'

location: location

properties: {

addressSpace: {

addressPrefixes: ['10.0.0.0/16']

}

subnets: [

{

name: 'web-subnet'

properties: {

addressPrefix: '10.0.1.0/24'

}

}

]

}
```

```
}
```

Deploy using:

```
az deployment group create \
—resource-group MyRG \
—template-file main.bicep
```

Blogs and Technical Communities

Microsoft Tech Community

The **Azure Networking Blog** is regularly updated with product announcements, previews, and use case breakdowns:

- https://techcommunity.microsoft.com/t5/azure-networking-blog/bg-p/AzureNetworking

Topics include:

- New features in Azure Firewall and Application Gateway
- Architecture walkthroughs for hybrid and multi-region solutions
- Troubleshooting deep dives

Azure Updates

Stay current with new networking features and roadmap items:

- https://azure.microsoft.com/en-us/updates/

Use filters for "Networking" category to focus your feed.

Forums

- **Microsoft Q&A**: Official forum for getting support from Microsoft engineers and the community.

  https://learn.microsoft.com/en-us/answers/topics/azure-networking.html

- **Stack Overflow**: Tag-specific questions and answers. Tags include azure-networking, vnet, nsg, and more.

- **Reddit**: r/AZURE offers community-driven discussions and practical insights.

Books and Publications

- *Microsoft Azure Networking: The Definitive Guide* by David Okeyode

  A detailed breakdown of Azure networking with use cases and architectural patterns.

- *Exam Ref AZ-700 Designing and Implementing Microsoft Azure Networking Solutions*

  A must-read for those pursuing the AZ-700 exam, full of practical examples and assessments.

- *Cloud Networking Simplified*

Offers cross-platform comparisons between AWS, GCP, and Azure—useful for architects working in hybrid/ multi-cloud environments.

Tools and Utilities

Azure Resource Graph Explorer

Use queries to explore and audit networking configurations across your environment.

Resources

| where type =~ 'microsoft.network/networksecuritygroups'

| project name, location, properties.securityRules

Azure Pricing Calculator

Estimate the cost of networking components such as ExpressRoute, Load Balancers, and VPN Gateways:

- https://azure.microsoft.com/en-us/pricing/calculator/

Network Watcher Tools

Access via portal or CLI to analyze traffic:

- Connection troubleshoot
- Packet capture
- Topology viewer

Events and Certifications

Stay involved through:

- **Microsoft Ignite**
- **Azure OpenHack**
- **Local Meetup Groups**
- **Cloud Skills Challenges** (often with free certification vouchers)

You can track events via the **Microsoft Events Hub**:

- https://events.microsoft.com/

Summary

Learning Azure networking is a continuous journey that goes beyond reading—hands-on experience, community engagement, certification preparation, and staying updated on new features are key. Whether you're deploying VNets for the first time or architecting a global network backbone, the resources listed here provide the structure, support, and scalability to sharpen your skills and achieve expertise in Microsoft Azure networking.

Sample Projects and Code Snippets

This section provides a comprehensive collection of sample projects and reusable code snippets designed to help you apply Azure Virtual Networking concepts in real-world scenarios. Each sample project demonstrates a practical use case, from building a secure multi-tier application to automating the deployment of hybrid networks. Code snippets are included to accelerate development, reduce configuration errors, and offer reference implementations that you can adapt to your own environments.

Sample Project 1: Multi-Tier Web Application in a Hub-and-Spoke Architecture

Objective

Deploy a scalable, secure web application with separate tiers for the frontend, application logic, and backend databases using a hub-and-spoke topology.

Components

- **Hub VNet** with shared services (firewall, Bastion, monitoring)
- **Spoke VNets** for frontend, app, and data tiers
- **VNet peering** between spokes and hub
- **NSGs and route tables** for segmentation
- **Private Endpoints** for storage and SQL

Bicep Template Overview

param location string = resourceGroup().location

resource hubVnet 'Microsoft.Network/virtualNetworks@2021-03-01' = {

name: 'hub-vnet'

```
location: location
properties: {
addressSpace: {
addressPrefixes: ['10.0.0.0/16']
}
subnets: [
{
name: 'AzureFirewallSubnet'
properties: {
addressPrefix: '10.0.0.0/24'
}
}
]
}
}
```

This project allows teams to enforce separation of concerns, apply Zero Trust principles, and establish a foundation for growth into hybrid or multi-region architectures.

Sample Project 2: Secure API Gateway with Azure Application Gateway and WAF

Objective

Expose a set of internal APIs securely to the internet using Application Gateway with WAF, protecting against OWASP Top 10 vulnerabilities.

Key Features

- **Application Gateway (v2)**
- **WAF policy with custom rules**
- **Path-based routing to backend pools**
- **Private backend pool VMs or App Services**

Configuration Highlights

az network application-gateway create \

—name ApiAppGateway \

—resource-group NetRG \

—location eastus \

—capacity 2 \

—sku WAF_v2 \

—vnet-name hub-vnet \

—subnet AppGatewaySubnet \

—frontend-port 443 \

—http-settings-cookie-based-affinity Enabled

WAF Custom Rule

az network application-gateway waf-policy custom-rule create \

—policy-name SecureApiPolicy \

—resource-group NetRG \

—rule-name BlockBadBots \

—priority 100 \

—rule-type MatchRule \

—match-conditions match-variables=RequestHeaders \

—operator Contains \

—values "BadBot"

This project ensures secure access while allowing for load balancing and future scaling.

Sample Project 3: Site-to-Site VPN for Hybrid Network

Objective

Connect an on-premises datacenter to an Azure VNet using a Site-to-Site VPN.

Infrastructure

- **VPN Gateway**
- **Local Network Gateway**
- **Connection with shared key**
- **Dynamic routing with BGP (optional)**

Key Commands

Create public IP

az network public-ip create \

—name VpnGatewayPublicIP \

—resource-group NetRG \

—allocation-method Dynamic

Create VPN Gateway

az network vpn-gateway create \

—name MyVpnGateway \

—public-ip-address VpnGatewayPublicIP \

—resource-group NetRG \

—vnet hub-vnet \

—gateway-type Vpn \

—vpn-type RouteBased \

```
—sku VpnGw1

# Create local network gateway

az network local-gateway create \

—resource-group NetRG \

—name OnPremGateway \

—gateway-ip-address 52.100.10.10 \

—local-address-prefixes 192.168.0.0/16

# Create connection

az network vpn-connection create \

—name OnPremToAzureConnection \

—resource-group NetRG \

—vnet-gateway1 MyVpnGateway \

—local-gateway2 OnPremGateway \

—shared-key "YourSharedKey"
```

This configuration supports hybrid workloads and enables seamless migration or expansion into Azure.

Sample Project 4: End-to-End Monitoring of Network Traffic

Objective

Enable diagnostics, NSG flow logs, and alerting for network monitoring and compliance auditing.

Setup

- **Enable Network Watcher**
- **Enable NSG flow logs**
- **Send logs to Log Analytics**
- **Create alerts for anomalies**

Example CLI Commands

az network watcher configure \

—locations eastus \

—enabled true \

—resource-group NetRG

az network watcher flow log configure \

—nsg MyAppNSG \

—enabled true \

—retention 7 \

—storage-account mystorageacct \

—resource-group NetRG \

—traffic-analytics true \

—workspace mystorageworkspace

Sample Alert Rule

az monitor metrics alert create \

—name NSGBlockedTraffic \

—resource-group NetRG \

—scopes /subscriptions/xxxx/resourceGroups/NetRG/providers/Microsoft.Network/networkSecurityGroups/MyAppNSG \

—condition "total NSGFlowLogs | where Action == 'Deny'" \

—description "Alert on denied traffic"

This project helps meet audit requirements and detect potential security threats.

Sample Project 5: Global Load Balancing with Azure Front Door

Objective

Distribute traffic across applications hosted in multiple regions to improve latency and resilience.

Tools

- **Azure Front Door Standard/Premium**
- **Backend pools per region**
- **Health probes**
- **Geo-filtering rules**

Front Door Deployment

az network front-door create \

—name GlobalFrontDoor \

—resource-group NetRG \

—backend-addresses eastusapp.azurewebsites.net westusapp.azurewebsites.net \

—accepted-protocols Https \

—frontend-endpoints myappfrontend

Health probes ensure regional failover in case of outage, and rules can be configured for throttling or A/B testing.

Sample Project 6: Secure Dev/Test Environment with Azure Bastion and JIT

Objective

Provide developers secure access to virtual machines for testing without exposing them to the public internet.

Components

- **Azure Bastion**
- **Just-in-Time VM Access**
- **NSGs blocking all public inbound traffic**

Key Steps

1. Deploy VMs with no public IP.
2. Enable Bastion host in the same VNet.
3. Configure JIT access via Azure Security Center.

az network bastion create \

—name DevBastion \

—public-ip-address DevBastionIP \

—resource-group NetRG \

—vnet-name dev-vnet \

—location eastus

Configure JIT:

az security jit-policy create \

—resource-group NetRG \

—location eastus \

—name DevVMAccess \

—virtual-machines "/subscriptions/xxxx/resourceGroups/NetRG/providers/Microsoft.Compute/virtualMachines/DevVM1"

This setup ensures a secure, auditable environment for development and testing.

Best Practices for Reusing Code Snippets

- **Parameterize everything**: Use variables for IP ranges, names, and locations.
- **Modularize your code**: Break down templates and scripts into reusable modules.
- **Version control**: Store your scripts in Git with proper commit messages and change tracking.
- **Integrate with pipelines**: Use Azure DevOps or GitHub Actions to automate deployments.
- **Validate before deployment**: Use az deployment what-if or Bicep's bicep build to preview changes.

Summary

These sample projects and code snippets demonstrate practical applications of Azure Virtual Networking and provide you with a toolbox for building secure, scalable, and compliant infrastructure. From simple VNet deployments to complex global architectures, using templates and automation ensures consistency, reduces manual errors, and accelerates development. Use these samples as a foundation, customize them to suit your environment, and continuously expand your library as Azure evolves.

API Reference Guide

This section provides a comprehensive guide to the most commonly used Azure networking APIs, command-line tools, and SDKs. These APIs are critical for automation, integration, and programmatic management of Azure network resources. Whether you're working with REST APIs directly, scripting with Azure CLI, or using SDKs in your favorite programming language, this reference will serve as a powerful foundation to streamline your development workflows and infrastructure provisioning.

Azure REST API Overview

Azure exposes a robust set of RESTful APIs that allow full control over network resources. These APIs follow standard HTTP semantics and support operations such as GET, PUT, POST, DELETE, and PATCH.

Base URL Format

https://management.azure.com/
subscriptions/{subscriptionId}/resourceGroups/{resourceGroupName}/p
Microsoft.Network/{resourceType}/{resourceName}?api-version={apiVe

Common Headers

Authorization: Bearer <access_token>

Content-Type: application/json

Tokens can be acquired using Azure CLI:

az account get-access-token—resource https://management.azure.com

Sample REST API Calls

Create a Virtual Network

Endpoint:

PUT
/subscriptions/{subscriptionId}/resourceGroups/{resourceGroupName}/p
Microsoft.Network/virtualNetworks/
myVNet?api-version=2021-03-01

Payload:

{

"location": "eastus",

"properties": {

"addressSpace": {

"addressPrefixes": ["10.0.0.0/16"]

},

"subnets": [

{

"name": "default",

"properties": {

"addressPrefix": "10.0.0.0/24"

}

}

```
]
}
}
```

Get NSG Rules

```
GET
/subscriptions/{subscriptionId}/resourceGroups/{resourceGroupName}/
Microsoft.Network/networkSecurityGroups/myNSG/
securityRules?api-version=2021-02-01
```

This returns a list of all defined security rules for the specified NSG.

Azure CLI Reference

Azure CLI (az) is a cross-platform command-line tool for managing Azure resources. It wraps the REST API in a human-friendly syntax and is perfect for scripting.

Create a VNet

```
az network vnet create \
—name MyVNet \
—resource-group MyRG \
—location eastus \
—address-prefix 10.0.0.0/16 \
—subnet-name default \
—subnet-prefix 10.0.0.0/24
```

List All Peered VNets

az network vnet peering list \

—resource-group MyRG \

—vnet-name MyVNet

Create Route Table

az network route-table create \

—name MyRouteTable \

—resource-group MyRG \

—location eastus

Add a Custom Route

az network route-table route create \

—resource-group MyRG \

—route-table-name MyRouteTable \

—name routeToFirewall \

—address-prefix 0.0.0.0/0 \

—next-hop-type VirtualAppliance \

—next-hop-ip-address 10.0.1.4

PowerShell Cmdlets Reference

Azure PowerShell is a powerful automation toolkit particularly useful in Windows-based environments or DevOps pipelines.

Create NSG and Rule

New-AzNetworkSecurityGroup -Name "WebNSG" -ResourceGroupName "MyRG" -Location "EastUS"

$rule = New-AzNetworkSecurityRuleConfig `

-Name "AllowWeb" `

-Description "Allow HTTP" `

-Access Allow `

-Protocol Tcp `

-Direction Inbound `

-Priority 100 `

-SourceAddressPrefix * `

-SourcePortRange * `

-DestinationAddressPrefix * `

-DestinationPortRange 80

$nsg = Get-AzNetworkSecurityGroup -Name "WebNSG" -ResourceGroupName "MyRG"

$nsg.SecurityRules.Add($rule)

Set-AzNetworkSecurityGroup -NetworkSecurityGroup $nsg

Retrieve VNet Information

```
Get-AzVirtualNetwork -Name "MyVNet" -ResourceGroupName "MyRG"
```

Azure SDKs

Azure provides SDKs for multiple programming languages, including:

- **Python**
- **JavaScript/TypeScript**
- **.NET (C#)**
- **Go**
- **Java**

These SDKs offer strongly typed client libraries that abstract the REST API.

Example: Python SDK to Create a VNet

```
from azure.identity import DefaultAzureCredential

from azure.mgmt.network import NetworkManagementClient

credential = DefaultAzureCredential()

client = NetworkManagementClient(credential, subscription_id)

async_vnet_creation = client.virtual_networks.begin_create_or_update(
```

```
"MyRG",
"MyVNet",
{
"location": "eastus",
"address_space": {
"address_prefixes": ["10.0.0.0/16"]
}
}
)
vnet = async_vnet_creation.result()
```

Example: JavaScript SDK to List NSGs

```
const { NetworkManagementClient } = require("@azure/arm-network");
const { DefaultAzureCredential } = require("@azure/identity");
const client = new NetworkManagementClient(new DefaultAzureCredential(), subscriptionId);
async function listNSGs() {
const result = await client.networkSecurityGroups.list("MyRG");
console.log(result);
}
```

listNSGs();

Postman and REST Clients

For testing APIs quickly:

1. Import Azure REST API collection into Postman.
2. Use the OAuth 2.0 authorization flow with Azure AD.
3. Token endpoint: https://login.microsoftonline.com/{tenantId}/oauth2/token
4. Set client_id, client_secret, and resource to https://management.azure.com/.

This allows interactive testing of networking APIs like creating subnets, managing routes, or peering VNets.

ARM Template Snippets

ARM templates provide a declarative way to define Azure infrastructure as JSON.

Example: Define a VNet and Subnet

```
{
"type": "Microsoft.Network/virtualNetworks",
"apiVersion": "2021-02-01",
"name": "MyVNet",
"location": "[resourceGroup().location]",
"properties": {
```

```
"addressSpace": {
"addressPrefixes": ["10.0.0.0/16"]
},
"subnets": [
{
"name": "web-subnet",
"properties": {
"addressPrefix": "10.0.1.0/24"
}
}
]
}
}
```

ARM templates are commonly used in CI/CD pipelines and support modularization through linked templates.

Bicep Module Samples

Bicep is the modern DSL for ARM, offering cleaner syntax and better modular support.

Bicep: Network Security Group

```
resource nsg 'Microsoft.Network/networkSecurityGroups@2022-01-01' = {
```

```
name: 'web-nsg'
location: resourceGroup().location
properties: {
securityRules: [
{
name: 'AllowHTTP'
properties: {
priority: 100
direction: 'Inbound'
access: 'Allow'
protocol: 'Tcp'
sourcePortRange: '*'
destinationPortRange: '80'
sourceAddressPrefix: '*'
destinationAddressPrefix: '*'
}
}
]
}
}
```

Use bicep build to convert this to ARM JSON or az deployment group create to deploy directly.

Azure Graph Queries (Kusto)

For querying network resources at scale:

Resources

| where type == "microsoft.network/virtualnetworks"

| project name, location, properties.addressSpace

This helps audit resource configurations across subscriptions.

Summary

Azure's APIs, CLI tools, and SDKs provide rich, programmable access to networking features that enable rapid deployment, consistent configurations, and seamless automation. This reference guide consolidates core usage patterns and templates, empowering you to manage networks effectively at scale. Whether you prefer scripting, coding, or REST API interactions, Azure provides the flexibility needed for enterprise networking operations.

Frequently Asked Questions

This section compiles a wide range of frequently asked questions (FAQs) related to Azure Virtual Networking. These questions are based on real-world use cases, community forums, certification topics, and troubleshooting scenarios. Whether you're a beginner deploying your first VNet or an architect designing hybrid networks, this FAQ is a valuable quick-reference guide to common challenges and best practices.

What is the difference between a VNet and a subnet?

A **Virtual Network (VNet)** is a logically isolated network in Azure that allows you to securely connect Azure resources. A **subnet** is a range of IP addresses within a VNet that segments the network to organize and secure resources.

- VNets can span availability zones but not regions.
- Subnets are used to apply security rules (NSGs), associate route tables, and segment workloads (e.g., web, app, data tiers).

Can I peer VNets across regions?

Yes. Azure supports **Global VNet Peering**, allowing you to connect VNets across different Azure regions.

- Latency is low and uses Microsoft's backbone network.
- You must configure peering on both VNets.
- Transitive peering is **not** supported (you must explicitly peer each VNet pair).

```
az network vnet peering create \

—name EastToWest \

—resource-group RG-East \

—vnet-name EastVNet \
```

```
—remote-vnet /subscriptions/<sub-id>/resourceGroups/
RG-West/providers/Microsoft.Network/virtualNetworks/
WestVNet \

—allow-vnet-access
```

How do I restrict internet access to Azure VMs?

To block internet access:

1. Do not assign public IP addresses.
2. Use NSGs to deny outbound internet traffic (e.g., 0.0.0.0/0).
3. Use route tables to override system routes, directing traffic to **Azure Firewall** or a **NAT Gateway**.

Example NSG outbound rule:

```
az network nsg rule create \

—resource-group MyRG \

—nsg-name MyNSG \

—name BlockInternet \

—priority 100 \

—direction Outbound \

—access Deny \

—protocol '*' \

—destination-port-range '*' \

—destination-address-prefixes Internet
```

How can I monitor traffic within a VNet?

Use **Azure Network Watcher**, which provides tools such as:

- **NSG Flow Logs**
- **Connection Monitor**
- **Topology View**
- **IP Flow Verify**

Enable flow logs for a Network Security Group:

az network watcher flow-log configure \

—resource-group MyRG \

—nsg-name MyNSG \

—enabled true \

—storage-account mystorageaccount \

—traffic-analytics true \

—workspace myloganalyticsworkspace

What is the best practice for VNet address space design?

Plan with scalability and segmentation in mind:

- Use /**16** CIDR blocks for VNets (10.x.0.0/16)
- Allocate /**24** subnets (10.x.y.0/24) to avoid waste

- Reserve address ranges for peering, gateways, and future use
- Avoid overlapping IPs between VNets or with on-premises networks

Use Azure IP address planning tools and worksheets during initial architecture design.

What's the difference between Service Endpoints and Private Endpoints?

Feature	Service Endpoints	Private Endpoints
Access Type	Over Azure backbone	Private IP in your VNet
DNS	Uses public DNS	Uses private DNS zone
Resources	Public resource IP, scoped to subnet	Private IP mapped to resource
Security	NSGs supported	More granular, private traffic

Recommendation: Use **Private Endpoints** for maximum security and compliance.

Can I connect VNets across subscriptions?

Yes. You can peer VNets across different subscriptions and even tenants (with proper permissions):

- Ensure that both subscriptions are in the same Azure Active Directory (or have appropriate role assignments).
- Peering configuration must be done on **both sides**.

Example:

```
az network vnet peering create \
—name PeerToPartner \
—resource-group RG1 \
—vnet-name VNet1 \
—remote-vnet /subscriptions/<other-sub-id>/resourceGroups/RG2/providers/Microsoft.Network/virtualNetworks/VNet2 \
—allow-vnet-access
```

How do I connect an on-premises network to Azure?

There are three main options:

1. **Point-to-Site VPN** – for developers or remote workers.
2. **Site-to-Site VPN** – connects entire on-prem networks to Azure VNets.
3. **ExpressRoute** – private, high-throughput connection suitable for production and compliance workloads.

VPN Gateways require a special subnet called GatewaySubnet.

```
az network vnet subnet create \
—name GatewaySubnet \
—resource-group MyRG \
—vnet-name MyVNet \
—address-prefix 10.0.255.0/27
```

Can Azure automatically route traffic between subnets?

Yes, Azure provides **system routes** that automatically handle traffic within a VNet. You can override these using **User-Defined Routes (UDRs)** for:

- Forced tunneling
- Next-hop to Azure Firewall or NVA
- Custom inter-subnet routing

```
az network route-table route create \
—resource-group MyRG \
—route-table-name MyRouteTable \
—name RouteToFirewall \
—address-prefix 0.0.0.0/0 \
—next-hop-type VirtualAppliance \
—next-hop-ip-address 10.0.1.4
```

How do I enforce Zero Trust in networking?

Zero Trust Networking involves:

- **NSGs** and **ASGs** to limit lateral movement
- **Private Endpoints** instead of public IPs
- **Azure Firewall** or **WAF** for perimeter control

- **Just-in-Time (JIT) VM Access** and **Azure Bastion** for secure admin access
- **Azure Policy** to enforce network rules and compliance

How do I troubleshoot connectivity between two Azure VMs?

Use **Network Watcher's Connection Troubleshoot** feature.

1. Enable Network Watcher in your region
2. Run the test via CLI or portal

az network watcher connection-monitor test-configuration create \

—resource-group MyRG \

—name MyTest \

—location eastus \

—source-resource MyVM1 \

—destination-address 10.1.0.4 \

—protocol TCP \

—destination-port 443

Review results to identify routing issues, NSG blocks, or DNS failures.

How many VNets can I have per region or subscription?

Azure imposes certain limits:

- 1,000 VNets per region per subscription (default)
- 500 VNet peerings per VNet (default)
- You can request quota increases via Azure support

Use the **Azure limits documentation** for up-to-date numbers:https://learn.microsoft.com/en-us/azure/azure-resource-manager/management/azure-subscription-service-limits

Can I use third-party firewalls in Azure?

Yes. Azure supports third-party **Network Virtual Appliances (NVAs)** such as Palo Alto, Fortinet, and Check Point.

- Deploy the NVA into a dedicated subnet
- Use route tables to direct traffic through the appliance
- Ensure throughput is sufficient for your workload

NVAs offer features beyond Azure Firewall, like IPS, advanced threat protection, and custom rule engines.

Is it possible to apply conditional access based on IP location?

Yes. **Azure Active Directory Conditional Access** policies allow restrictions based on:

- Named locations (specific IPs or countries)
- Device compliance
- User risk levels

Example use case: only allow access to Azure Portal from corporate IP ranges.

Can I automate network deployments?

Absolutely. You can use:

- **ARM Templates**
- **Bicep**
- **Terraform**
- **Pulumi**
- **Azure CLI / PowerShell scripts**
- **Azure DevOps or GitHub Actions** pipelines

Example Bicep deployment:

```
param location string

resource vnet 'Microsoft.Network/virtualNetworks@2022-01-01' = {

name: 'myVnet'

location: location

properties: {

addressSpace: {

addressPrefixes: ['10.0.0.0/16']

}
```

```
}
}
```

Summary

These FAQs address a broad spectrum of Azure Virtual Networking challenges, from foundational setup to advanced scenarios. Bookmark this section as a ready-reference for troubleshooting, planning, and implementation. Azure networking is a deep and evolving domain—continue to experiment, automate, and leverage Microsoft's documentation and tools to stay current and efficient.

www.ingramcontent.com/pod-product-compliance
Lightning Source LLC
LaVergne TN
LVHW090303210926
848480LV00001B/116